SCRAP THE PAST, LEARN FROM IT
BUT START FROM SCRATCH USING **MUST**
THE "KISS" PRINCIPLE!

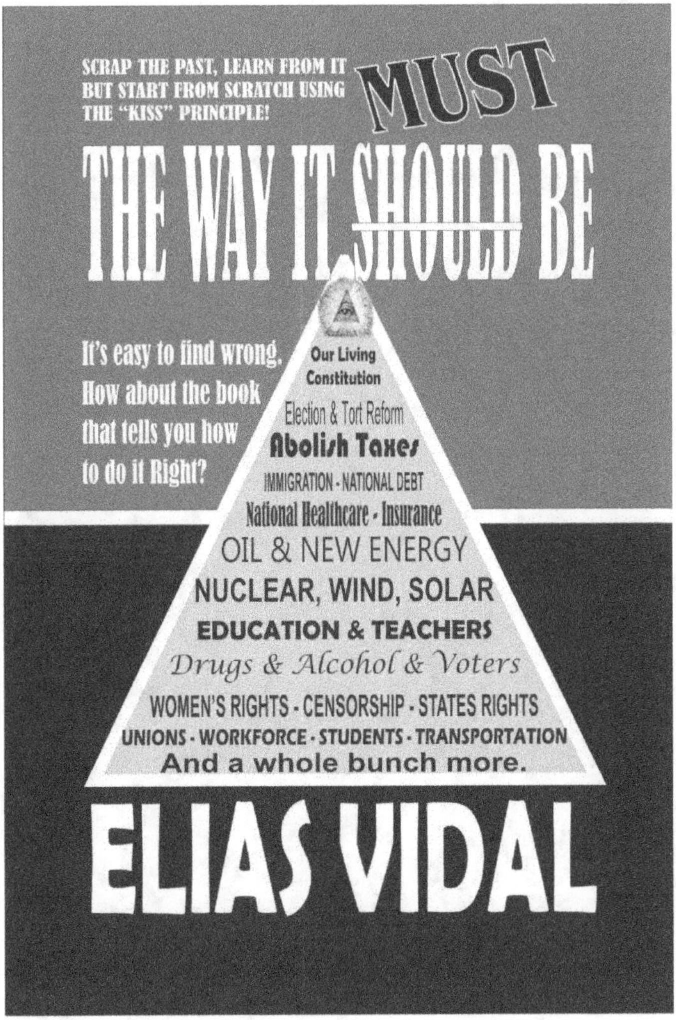

THE WAY IT ~~SHOULD~~ BE

It's easy to find wrong.
How about the book
that tells you how
to do it Right?

Our Living
Constitution

Election & Tort Reform

Abolish Taxes

IMMIGRATION - NATIONAL DEBT

National Healthcare - Insurance

OIL & NEW ENERGY

NUCLEAR, WIND, SOLAR

EDUCATION & TEACHERS

Drugs & Alcohol & Voters

WOMEN'S RIGHTS - CENSORSHIP - STATES RIGHTS

UNIONS - WORKFORCE - STUDENTS - TRANSPORTATION

And a whole bunch more.

ELIAS VIDAL

THE WAY IT ~~SHOULD~~ **MUST** BE

ALTA PUBLISHING

P. O. Box 2141
California City, CA 93504
760.373.8227 / 760.578.6258
Toll Free Fax: 877.842.3052
editor@ap4books.com

THE WAY IT ~~SHOULD~~ **MUST** BE

Scrap It All & Start From Scratch!
It's almost too late to fix the mess we are in.

THE WAY IT ~~SHOULD~~ MUST BE©

THE LITTLE BOOK THAT CAN

It's easy to find wrong!
How about a book that tells you
How to do it right?

By

ELIAS VIDAL

Edited by
Rosanne Mork

Copyright - June 2011-2012

Published by

ALTA PUBLISHING LLC
P.O. Box 411
Woodland Hills, CA 91365

TABLE OF CONTENTS:

INTRODUCTION:

For some, this book is going to be hard to take. At times it will seem that it has been written by a moron, or a maniac, who has no clue about the things he writes. I guess it is perfectly understandable because there are only a few million people in this world who can think like me, like us.

I have been thinking about these solutions for many years. There is not one day that goes by that I don't reflect on the things I have written so far to make sure that I am onto something. Regardless, some of these ideas will seem, to many, just outrageous, undoable, pretentious and simply dumb and impossible to put into effect.

  Notwithstanding the above, NOTHING is impossible, when you have an open mind and when you try, at every level of your life, to be pragmatic, rational and KEEP IT SIMPLE!

Every day, we are bombarded by bad news (because good news does not sell, I'm told) from television, radio, newspaper articles and magazines, and of course through the thousands of readily available, Blogs, Facebook, Twitters, plus everything imaginable through the internet. We are hit with countless "Alerts" and "News Flash" headlines depicting dire news items, and we sit there and soak it all in, often wondering why things can't get better.

WARNING: If you are expecting a "heady," brainy dissertation, pseudo-intellectual answers of what all our problems are and how to solve them, you picked up the wrong book. You're not getting that here. I'm not writing this book to impress other writers, the literati, Wall Street, Madison Avenue, the Hollywood crowd or even Steven Spielberg (well maybe a little for Steven).

I'm writing this book for guys like me and my friends, who don't want the garbage spewed on those PBS political shows or on Fox, ABC, CNN, et. al.

Some of the solutions to the problems can be so simple, so easy and based on common sense, that I often wonder why people make things so complicated.

A POSSIBLE ANSWER: Is it because politicians, administrators, lawyers, television producers and such just don't want to make it easy for the average person to grasp and understand the problems, thereby accomplishing their goal of "hooking" us into watching, hearing, or reading their stuff? If so, they underestimate most of us.

If you are like me, I often find myself yelling at the television or screaming at the "talking head" on the radio. "How can they spew such silly babble? Do these people get paid for that?" Even worse, you see and hear our elected politicians spewing the same rubbish and acting as if they know what's good for us. "Is he for real," I often scream. "He doesn't know shit!" or "She's so stupid, who put her in charge?"

My wife often jumps in with a clever tidbit of advice; "Relax, you're going to have a heart attack." Or "Do you think those people will listen to you? They have their ulterior motives, and you know that." But the one comment she often makes that really brings my blood to the boiling point is when she often says, "No one will listen to us. Just try to make the best of it."

Well, my dear, I won't! And I'll go down with the ship fighting.

For years, I've been thinking of solutions, simple solutions that can help our country. Right off the top of my head there is an easy answer, when Shakespeare once said and wrote, "Kill the lawyers." I agree in principle. When you look at most of our problems here in the United States, there's always a lawyer or two, heavily involved, embroiled and ensconced in the middle of the argument. Who wins? THE LAWYERS of course! Nice gig if you can get it.

Time and again, I've sat down and jotted notes on just about everything topical, especially political issues that need to be resolved in the 21st Century.

When I start analyzing such problems, it always comes down to one thing, politicians will never go out on the limb to resolves issues, because **they want to be reelected**, and to do that, you can't be too creative, too simplistic, and too fair-minded. You must try to reach the lowest common denominator (large masses) to get elected or reelected. What a bunch of bull crap that is.

Therefore, after all these years of stewing about a number of things, I finally decided to write a book about what I perceive to be "simple" solutions to almost every problem we face. I don't dilute myself in thinking that anyone is going to read these simplistic answers and right away go out and become my disciples, especially, not politicians, lawyers and government employees who are simply going to hate the first few chapters in the book.

I believe that there are a lot of people like me who are just fed up with what is going on in our country. As we see crisis after crisis, most of our politicians and career bureaucrats seem oblivious. I also understand that the *"Devil is in the details,"* which means that there are a lot more impediments to consider before accepting my approach, but these are not insurmountable.

In reading this book, please keep in mind that in order to achieve one goal, sometimes others have to precede them. That's why I've illustrated the subject matters using the "Pyramid" structure. Firstly, certain things have to happen before the next one makes sense and can be accomplished.

Finally, I realize that I have left out some topics that you, the reader, consider important to be addressed. However, I can only cover those that seem to pop out at me from my tiny muscle between my ears. It's up to you to take the lead on those items that really bug you and are not covered here. You can even send those peeves to us and maybe we will include them on our second edition to this book.

So before I die and become potting soil to the world, I have to get these problem-solving ideas off my chest, on paper and hope for the best.

Elias Vidal

* "Simple" is on the brain of the beholder, and since my brain is rather uncomplicated, only an easy answer works for me."

My motto: ***"If you can dream it, it is possible."***

CHAPTER 1

OUR LIVING CONSTITUTION
(As it was written, with spelling anomalies and all…)

We the People of the United States, *in Order to form a more perfect Union, establish Justice, insure domestic Tranquility, provide for the common defense, promote the general Welfare, and secure the Blessings of Liberty to ourselves and our Posterity, do ordain and establish this Constitution for the United States of America…"*

So as not to lose you in just a few pages, the entire Constitution can be found in the back of this book. You should read and even try to memorize parts of it because nowadays it is important to be knowledgeable of your rights and the way this country should be run.

The Constitution begins with: *"We the People."* There is so much wisdom in that simple phrase, that most people do not understand what the framers of our constitution meant. Our

Founding Fathers penned those words as pent-up souls yearning for liberation, in ink steeped with years of persecution, disenfranchising, slavery, and oppression.

By the Grace of God, thirty-nine citizens framed the infamous Constitution of the United States in this environment of persecution. Seven men are often labeled the "Founding Fathers," including: Benjamin Franklin, George Washington, John Adams, Thomas Jefferson, John Jay *(why don't we ever hear about him?)*, James Madison and Alexander Hamilton.

These men, along with thirty-two others created a document that still stands as the standard for Democracy. It is the template of freedom and is often adapted as a model by other nations. Our Constitution has seen twenty-seven "amendments" since 1789; thus making it a "living document" that evolves with our nation's progress.

If we want to restore our form of governance and the American way of life to what the Founding Fathers intended, major changes must be made NOW! We totter on the brink of social, economic, cultural and political oblivion.

Tell me that I'm wrong and I'll submit the evidence that just this morning, I heard on the news that our current Administration's Education Department is thinking of teaching sixth graders in our public school system about oral sex, the "dog" position, masturbation, and other adult topics. And what is the response of many educators? There are hundreds of teachers signing up to teach this course! Are they nuts? No, I'm not against free speech or AGAINST thinking outside the box. I just think that certain things, basic Christian values, should remain in our lives. Just because some misguided person thinks that oral sex was nothing more than a kiss, even if he is the holder of the most powerful office in this country, does not make it right. It's just convenient.

It is sad and disturbing that when I speak with parents and young couples, only a few are aware of this proposed change in the teaching curriculum. They act totally surprised when I mention what it is currently proposed and what the ramifications attached to such change would mean to their children and to society in General. Their mouths drop and they say, "We can't allow this to happen."

Yet there are others who feel, for example, that oral copulation is nothing more than a kiss. It's not really sex.

One person noted that if it was that bad they would have convicted President Clinton of obscene and lascivious behavior, but they didn't. Their sense of right and wrong is based on what they watched on TV. The pundits dismissed such actions; so do parents. Unbelievable!

What I'm proposing in this book is that we amend our Constitution IMMEDIATELY before it is too late! Yes, it takes a behemoth effort from Congress to bring amendments to the floor; especially paradigm changes that will put politicians and their staffs out of a job after their one term is over.

But it is for the good of this country that we must accept new and progressive ways of governance. We have to start somewhere, so why not now; let's roll up our collective sleeves and begin, shall we?

CHAPTER 2

Term Limits for EVERYONE –
From the Top on Down!

OK, where do many of our problems begin? I dare say that the ills we experience in our daily lives derive from our current possible double-term limit for the President. Think I'm crazy? Just read on…

From the President of the United States to U.S. Senators, U.S. Congresspersons, to your state, city and local governments, career politicians press to be elected or re-elected to the limit of the law. Except for those few persons of principle who just *"had it"* after one term.

For other so called public-servants, getting elected is like sniffing an aphrodisiac, taking a hit off a joint, or shooting up the veins. One gets hooked and there's nothing more or less to say about it. They are addicted!

In the case of our current President, Barack Obama, after the first two years of his first term, he has already started raising support in both money and people (votes), and has assembled a campaign war chest designed to get him re-elected two years hence. Notice that he *is campaigning* two years before his term is up. Two years that he should be working 100% of the time for the nation and not his personal interest.

I estimate that as much as 40% of his time is spent figuring out re-election strategies and events. Presidents have a habit of using the "Bully Pulpit" to keep their jobs -- let's name it for what it is –inappropriate, disgusting and unsavory.

We don`t need to go too far to prove my point. President Barack Hussein Obama, as of mid-year 2011, has already amassed over eighty million dollars for his re-election.

How did he accomplish this? Certainly not by working every hour of the day for his country and for us, is it? Why did we send him to Washington if not to perform duties for our nation for the next four years?

While this country is going through the worst economic times ever since the depression; he and his party are deep in re-election mode. His calendar is loaded with functions designed to build up his war-chest for the upcoming 2012 elections.

On July 22, 2011, instead of making a speech on how to solve our current financial woes and deficits, curtail massive spending and rein in the growing unemployment rate (currently 8.2% as of July 2012 of the workforce or almost 30 million people!); he pointed fingers at everyone but himself. If you were from out of space, perhaps you would not catch it, but for the savvy viewer, his diatribe was merely a POLITICAL SPEECH of the first order!

Imagine, with our economy going down faster than feces in a toilet bowl (more so in California where we can only fill half the bowl), and smelling just as badly, he's already vying for re-election.

This extended example demonstrates why nothing good for the country will ever get done. Moreover the addictive power of holding office and the divisions and dissension within his party is a disaster in the making.

And who loses? **<u>WE DO FOLKS!</u>** We get the sucker punch squarely up our noses. The people of the United States take it on the chin for these self-involved clowns. They claim this is the American way of politics….if that is so, here's a better way.

The answer is: **KISS** or "**Keep It Simple Stupid**" (you'll see this acronym throughout the book because I believe what it stands for. Common sense leads the way.)

As mentioned earlier, it is time to amend the Constitution. It's time to modify term limits so that the President is elected for **<u>a one, six-year term with no possibility for re-election</u>**. Let me say that a different way: the President of the United States would have six years to make things happen and put his/her ideas and promises to work without having to worry about the party, re-election, or supporting other candidates.

From the day the President is elected and takes over the most powerful office in the world, he/she will have to work for an entire six years or 2,190 days (give and take a few days for Leap years), on nothing but the people's work.

When I say "nothing but the people's work" that's exactly what I mean.

In fact the amendment should go one step further. Once a President is elected as a Democrat, Republican, Independent, Libertarian, Green Peace, Greenie or whatever, he/she relinquishes party affiliation and becomes the first member and leader of the **"American Party!"**

Under this plan, the President no longer is tied to any political group except the one that he will work for 2,190 of his days for – *"We the People"* of the United States and no one else.

Can you smell what's coming next?

I admit that there are a lot of great people, with great ideas who get elected and go into office with every intention to do well and put their ideals to work. Why not? That's why they were elected in the first place. But when that person takes office, and I mean immediately, not two or three weeks later; their staff begins to assemble a re-election machine.

In the process, that well-meaning person rubs shoulders with a lot of people who are hoping to influence the elected politician to support their favorite cause – and the money starts pouring into the coffers. But the generosity of these people does not come without conditions. As they say, "There's no free lunch and there's no free money."

So what happens to those ideals that sounded so sincere during the political speeches and campaigns? What happened to that energy the candidate exuded and the claims to make things right in government by making a difference, and making changes for the betterment of our citizens, our country and the world? As I said before: "like feces in a toilet bowl…" You get what I mean.

Unfortunately, I do not know of a President in modern times who has not succumbed to these nasty habits, not a Republican or Democrat.

However, if you look back in history, President Polk was a unique individual. He announced to the nation that he was not interested in re-election and that he was going to do what he promised to do if elected; whether people liked it or not. People took him at his word and he served this country well for one, four-year term. Whether he did much good for the country or not (history really knows), he held true to his ideals and kept his word. You have to admire him for that.

Before violating my own KISS principle, let me stop going on and on and offer a <u>solution:</u>

1. Every national, state and local public service office should be for a one, six-year term without the possibility of re-election. From the Presidential Office of the United States, to the Senate (national and state), Congress (national and state) and all the way down to local city mayors, councilpersons, fire chief's, dog catchers, you name it…just one six-year term without the possibility of being reelected.
2. Once a person serves his/her six-year term, they cannot ever run again for the same office.
3. After a six year hiatus, that person may run for another office, also for one six year term.

4. Persons, who have served for six years, should be rated during subsequent elections. Accordingly, constituents, while voting for new candidates, will also have the opportunity to "rate" the previous civil servant as: (a)-excellent, (b)-very good, (c)-good, (d)-fair and (f)-poor, in order to set up the criteria for that politician's retirement and pension pay or future election into another office.

We do not need "career politicians." What we need are honest, creative people, who are willing to work hard for what they believe will be good for the community, the state and the nation. We need to send them to office to bring that vision to life during the period they were elected. If they cannot do it in six years, well maybe we sent the wrong person. What a fresh idea!

"We the People" will rate each civil servant's pension via popular vote. A politician's future income is only as good as how they've been rated by constituents. That will be reflected on their "pension" level until they die.
Now isn't that simple?

But what does all this mean? How will it affect the politico? That's also simple:

When a person does not have to worry about being re-elected, or helping someone else win an election, that person owes and is owned by no one.
He or she is free to do whatever is best for their constituents with absolutely no fear of losing the next election.

It's so simple that it scares me; though probably less than the average career politician. There must be something wrong with the idea; and I'm sure that there's plenty of room to improve it...but at this point and time, I'm happy with it as a starting point for change.

CHAPTER 3

Kill the Politician/Lawyers...
(Metaphorically Speaking)

"The first thing we do," said the character in Shakespeare's Henry VI is "kill all the lawyers." I do not profess to really "kill the lawyers" but to bar them from ever serving in public office. A lawyer working as politicians seems contrary to their oath to help people.

A lawyer in politics is tantamount to releasing a healthy bull in a herd of bovines in heat. The only one who comes out ahead and enjoys the herd is...the bull. In human analogy, everyone else feels used, left behind with just a glimpse, a glimmer of having had good times. Lawyers never really lose; one will just make a few more bucks than the other, that's all.

The idea of an attorney serving in politics is an oxymoron because practicing law is a self-serving profession. The politician-lawyer is impelled to complicate things to assure reelection and future employment. In addition, the more complicated the law is in its verbiage and volume, the easier it is for politician-lawyers to protect their interests in ways most people don't see or understand. Am I saying politician lawyers are self-serving? You betchaa!

While term limits and elections could cut short their tenure to politicians-lawyers, as prescribed on the previous chapter, I still want lawyers off the public rolls. They can be hired to interpret the law, give advice as to the legalities of new legislation, mandates, and proposed articles, but he/she should not serve as a public servant!

I'm not trying to cut off the legal profession at its knees, when it comes to politics, but there are sufficient examples of politicians wrapping their argument in legal terms so complicated that the average Joe or Jane has a hard time following it. There are sufficient problems in this country and in this world for legal minds to tackle and resolve – attorneys should stick to those and stay out of politics.

THE KISS PRINCIPLE?

1. Lawyers should never be politicians or run for office
2. Lawyers should help and advise politicians and bureaucrats as to the legalities of governance.

Why change so drastically, you ask?

As an example, here is part of those 77,000 pages of H.R. 3200 I.H (National Health Care law presented by President Obama), to the 111th Congress:

"SEC. 114. NONDISCRIMINATION IN BENEFITS; PARITY IN MENTAL *HEALTH AND SUBSTANCE ABUSE DISORDER BENEFITS.*

> *(a) Nondiscrimination in Benefits- A qualified health benefits plan shall comply with standards established by the Commissioner to prohibit discrimination in health benefits or benefit structures for qualifying health benefits plans, building from sections 702 of Employee Retirement Income Security Act of 1974, 2702 of the Public Health Service Act, and section 9802 of the Internal Revenue Code of 1986.*

Say what? It would take a constitutional attorney to understand what "building from sections 702 of Employee Retirement Income Security Act of 1974" is and even where to find it; then find the "2702 of the Public Health Service Act" and finally find "section 9802 of the Internal Revenue Code of 1986." Are you kidding me?

Laws should be written so that average people in this country can read and understand them.

Moreover, a law should be written with a particular subject in mind.

No other subject matter or "string" attachment should be added or amended. One law per item and that's all. None of this "piggy back" sliding a less popular or more controversial law with one law that is more benign and perhaps it is sure to pass.

Now that I've managed to piss off a lot of attorneys and would-be judges, why not upset more people in the legal profession. Do I dare say it? Yes, I will...it is time for

TORT REFORM!

CHAPTER 4

Tort Reform
(Laws are out of whack!)

There are truths and myths regarding tort reform in this country. You can read opinions on both sides of the argument and be convinced as to what they say. I've read these opposing positions and to be perfectly honest, I am as confused as ever about who is right and who is wrong!

Therefore, as the saying goes, I would rather err on the side of caution than make assertions that I don't really understand.

This much I know – there are TOO MANY LAWS! Again, it all goes back to politician-lawyers often writing laws so that the average Joe or Jane cannot ever hope to understand them.

Do you know that there are 200,000 pages in the federal register alone and an additional 72,536 pages just in the U.S. Tax Code books, according to the U.S. Government Printing Office?

The U.S. Code (i.e., the codified general statutes) with West's annotations is contained in 356 volumes and takes up 55 feet of shelf space! The Code itself, from the USGPO (United States Government Printing Office), is published in 35 volumes from around 1,200 to 1,400 pages each, including 6,850 pages of index in 6 volumes and one other volume that is nothing but a 1,400-page LIST of the other public laws that have not been codified (e.g., the budget, etc.). Confused?

Oh, but then there is an additional Code of Federal Regulations for another 20,000 pages. Check out the sources yourself:

http://bookstore.gpo.gov
and *http://west.thompson.com*

Many attorneys and CPA's don't even understand the myriad of laws and have to hire "specialists" who can explain the meaning, intent and interpretation! Is that ridiculous or what?

You know a long time ago I heard someone say on a radio show, that if we burned all our federal and state law books and started from scratch, we would have a better society; one that would understand the principles of living and working together. Is this too radical for you?

Obviously, I believe such an idea has merit.

Let's elect regular people for a six year term and judge their performance by popular vote and reward them for making laws that we can all understand and live with. Heck that sounds good to me. I can live with that. How about you?

Unfortunately, I find it hard to digest and live with our present laws since I cannot for the life of me, understand them completely. It is absolutely frustrating for a person with an average education, good moral principles and a large dose of common sense, to make anything out of the written rule.

Laws are written with legal verbiage intended to cover every possible situation. If I read three pages, I am absolutely lost and can't really make out what is being said...unless I call a lawyer of course, at a cost from $125 to $500 or $600 per hour. Who can afford to comply with our rules and regulations?

In Section C of the Federal Register (33647) – Section by Section Analysis of Rules and Regulations, it states:

"The rule does not contain a statement regarding a financial institution's ability to comply with the rule in ways other than as suggested in the examples, but does provide that the examples are not exclusive. The rule also states that compliance with the examples will constitute compliance with the rule. The Commission believes that, when read together, these provisions give financial institutions sufficient flexibility to comply with the regulation but also sufficient..."

And if that isn't enough, sneaky politician-lawyers manage to include into new laws something that has nothing to do with the intent of the law in the first place; all in the name of getting their pet legislation "piggybacked" onto new legislation.

For example as it was reported in a newspaper article: "For years, Illinoisans have watched, sometimes in amazement, as their lawmakers have sliced and diced bills, eventually jamming key measures that political leaders want passed into a single piece of legislation at the end of the session.

Last November, the General Assembly did just that, mixing a politically popular bill requiring police to tell the public when child-sex offenders move to town with a more volatile measure that some lawmakers feared could be portrayed as a state gasoline tax increase--a fee on gas distributors to pay for the cleanup of leaking underground petroleum tanks."

This was reported by staff writers Andrew Fagelman and Rick Pearson of the Chicago Tribune.

What does one thing have to do with the other? NOTHING! Yet the sneaky bastards tried to slide it under the watchful, yet bewildered eyes of the people. Luckily the courts deemed it unconstitutional and voted it down.

I can think of several words for that: Devious, dishonest, deceitful, fraudulent...or just another case of "politics as usual."

Tort Reform can come in many ways and heaven knows we need it. I would like to tackle one particular area for reform which affects almost every phase of life here in the United States. One cannot escape it or live without it, but only be better prepared to tackle it. What is it?

LIABILITY! The scariest word in the English language! Liability pressures everyone toward doing nothing in this country that might produce personal or corporate liability. Today, complementing a woman or making a remark about an individual can bring libelous consequences.

Liability issues are out of control and the lawyers have made it so.

Tell me how fair this is, in October 1998: *"A Terrence Dickson of Bristol, Pennsylvania was leaving a house he had just finished robbing by way of the garage. He was not able to get the garage door open since the automatic door opener was malfunctioning. He couldn't re-enter the house because the door connecting the house and garage locked when he pulled it shut. The family was on vacation. Mr. Dickson found himself locked in the garage for eight days. He subsided on a case of Pepsi he found, and a large bag of dry dog food. He sued the homeowner's insurance claiming the situation caused him undue mental anguish. The jury agreed to the tune of half a million dollars!"* This story was reported on the website, called Stella Awards.

The Los Angeles Times, in an article dated June 2001, reported that a liquor store owner had a thief come through his store's roof. In the course of committing this felonious act, the thief cut a hole in the roof of the store to get in, got stuck in the process, fell and broke his back. The so-call "victim" then sued the store owner for not having sufficient protection in place to keep someone like him (a thief) from getting into the store, crashing and hurting himself.

The courts ruled against the liquor store owner, and awarded the felon over a million dollars in punitive and compensatory damages. Are we out of our frikin' minds?

There are thousands such vulgarities in the legal record. But let me give one more example just to prove how far-fetched we are with our laws:

Two young men climbed over a twelve-foot chain link fence into a skateboard park after hours. The fence had "Danger" signs every ten feet and also warned of patrolling unleashed guard dogs. The owner of the skate park used due-diligence in protecting his property, while "protecting" would be intruders via the warning signs. One would think such warnings would be enough to deter people from entering.

As it happened, these two young men, ages 16 and 17, got over the fence and skated after hours in the moonlight for a few minutes until one of the Doberman Pinschers positioned itself on the other side of the inner park fence and barked. The two young men continued to skate knowing the dogs were on the other side and would not jump the fence.

But that wasn't enough. After they grew hot and tired, they plotted to break into a Coke machine to steal sodas. The free water next to the Coke machine was not good enough. So they climbed out of the skate park area and broke the glass on the Coke machine with one of their skateboards and grabbed a handful of cans, a whole bunch of coins and cash.

Suddenly a Doberman crawled over the fence and attacked one of them, knocked him to the ground and bit him on the leg and arm. Blood flowed. The other young man got away and went to get help.

A few minutes later, the police arrived, jumped the 12-foot fence (one of the officers got hung up on the top of the fence for a while), then shot the mulling dog and the other that was just standing nearby.

Did the young men get cited for breaking in? No.

Did the owner get a judgment against himself and the insurance company? Yes. Did they have to pay off for medical costs and psychological damages? Yes.

I was the owner of the facility.

The laws pertaining to this case were written, to say the least, in an ambiguous and complicated manner; but the way they were interpreted by the court was ludicrous. The judge told me that I had created an "attractive nuisance" which lured kids to it.

To this day, I truly believe the jury's judgment solely depended on what they had for breakfast and not what was a common sense decision. Isn't that preposterous?

I could fill hundreds of pages with ridiculous cases that put a dark cloud over our legal system and called to scrutiny how we either appoint or elect judges. There's definitely something wrong that needs to be corrected.

TORT REFORM in the area of LIABILITY must include a financial limit on ALL cases. Politicians (not attorneys) should craft laws with sensible, simple limits and still give options in the event of unique cases.

For example, if a plumber gets hurt on a job and is incapacitated for a time so that he/she cannot work, there should be a limit as to how much compensation is given if the defendant loses the case. A plumber who makes $100,000 a year should not get $10,000.000.00 in compensation and punitive damages.

Moreover, if a plumber is injured permanently and is disabled so that he/she cannot do any other job, a judge should be able to calculate what the person would have made the rest of his life as a plumber using current age, life expectancy and average wage: thus making a sensible and thought-out decision on a compensation award. That seems fair to me.

The effect of Tort Reform would be felt in all sectors of our economy. After all, why do doctors, hospitals, hotels, and car leasing companies, lawyers, accountants, and other professionals charge so much for their services?

Do you know that in most cases from 25% to 45% of their fee goes toward Liability and/or Product Liability insurance, in the event that they get sued?

Do you realize that every new item that you buy, including cars, trucks, bicycles, roller skates, clothing or even mattresses, have about the same percentage added to the retail price to cover "product liability" and liability in general?

The bottom line is that every phase of our life is practically affected and controlled by the law.

The law no longer protects us. Now we have to consider how to protect ourselves from the law and its application.

The irony of all ironies is that even lawyers have to buy "liability" or "malpractice" insurance because unscrupulous fellow attorneys may take a case that could severely financially ruin the former or drive him out of the profession.

I want politicians (the non-legal minds-type) to come up with sensible laws that are simple to interpret and uphold. I'm absolutely confident that this is possible. Nothing can be worse than the laws that have been written. So what do we have to lose?

The KISS Principle: I would like to see Federal and State laws condensed into simple language and be no longer than 100 pages. I would like to see the "meat and potatoes" of any law, clearly defined in one or two paragraphs, written NOT by lawyers but by people like you and me.

Too simplistic? What do you think?

CHAPTER 5

Taxes - Who Should Pay and Who Shouldn't?

Add up our current tax laws. The sum is seventy thousand pages and counting. Ridiculous! I dare say that only a handful of tax attorneys or CPA's (Certified Public Accountants) really understand every single line of the code. The other 99% think they do, but have to consult with many others because they don't know the law in its entirety and don't want to be held "liable" for erroneously advising others *(see, there goes that word again...liability).*

We all try to pay the least, so I will be the first to admit that I try in every way possible to not pay taxes, or at least not a penny more than I'm supposed to. And why? Two reasons:

1. I know others, especially those with lots of money and a gaggle of attorneys in their henhouse, will try in

every which way to keep their money from going for taxes. And...

2. Even when I pay my taxes, I know that as much as 80% of every dollar I send will be "pissed" away by our local, state and federal government. This can be likened to funding drunken sailors on a week-long leave.

There is no way I want to underwrite the waste of money. I work too hard to make and keep my money.   Living in the United States affords us the freedom to win or make lots of money and sometimes, to lose it.

SO WHAT IS THE SOLUTION?

<u>Let's get rid of all city, state and federal taxes.</u> No more FICA, Income Tax, no more deductions and no more April 15 filings!

No, this isn't Presidential candidate Cain's 9 - 9 - 9 tax proposal, because it doesn't go far enough. The proponents of the "Flat Tax" are closer to the answer but there is a better way.

For years I've heard rumors about the tax I'm proposing, but for the most part, the concept remains dormant. I've been a proponent of this type of tax for over thirty-years, since first hearing of it from a renowned economist. It actually was popularly introduced in the 1950s by France when it was trying to join the European Economic Community (EEC). But in 1973 Lord Barber, chancellor under Prime Minister Sir Edwin Heath, proposed a 10% tax across the board.

Unfortunately, people started picking at it and adding complexities of "exceptions and special deductions."

Lord Barber called it then the "**Value Added Tax**," but in the form I'm proposing now, I go one step further and I call it "**The Progressive Painless Tax Act.**"

Do you know why I like it? I like it because nobody is immune from paying their fair share. There is an exception that I will explain hereinafter; but even poor people must pay something, though in the end they will likely get part or all back. But I'm getting ahead here.

The "**The Progressive Painless Tax Act**" is the fairest tax of all because each person pays according to what they can afford to buy.

With the exception of certain staple foods: milk, bread, cereal and a few others - all other items should have "**The Progressive Painless Tax**" **(or TPPT)** of 10% included in the price. *(Note, I'm using the ten percent figure because it is easier for me to illustrate, but the percentage can be as low as 2% or as high as 15% or more - Economist can figure this out much better than I.)*

Here is the "progressive" angle that will serve well. Producers on down the line will start paying a 10% tax with the purchase of the "raw" material for the manufacture of a product. An additional 10% tax is charged at every step in the distribution process until the item reaches the retail outlet where the 10% TPPT is included.

By the time a product hits the retail level, that item has already generated several taxes to all levels of government without the consumer really knowing about it or feeling it: **"Painless!"**

Again, not being an economist, but putting some practical wisdom to work, I'm using the formula of "10% + 10% + 10% + 10%" across the board *(in order to make it easier to compute)*, which will generate sufficient taxes to fund every level of local, state and national government, as long as there is a "balanced budget" adopted by Congress. The TPPT percentage may need to be adjusted to perhaps a lower rate, but I will leave that determination to the numbers crunchers.

Based on the formula above (and taking into consideration published national retail numbers for 2010, **The Progressive Painless Tax** covers all our expenses with a few trillions in surplus for a rainy day.

Here is how I arrived at my proposition and I hope I don't bore you:

- Producer owns a large quarry of silica sand and he sells $10.00 worth to Manufacturer.
- Manufacturer pays Producer $10.00 plus 10% for taxes or a total of $11.00.
- The government takes **$1.00** out of the sale immediately into the bank, splitting it first with local, county, state and federal agencies.
- Manufacturer creates a beautiful vase and realizes that he has to get $14.00 for each vase to pay off labor, materials, time, etc. and make a profit.
- Therefore he sells the Distributor the vase for $14.00 plus 10% tax for a total of $15.40.
- The government collects **$1.40** in tax.
- The Distributor now hits the Retailer and makes a deal: $18.00 to carry the beautiful vase. Retailer thinks it's a good deal so he buys it for $18.00 plus tax.

- The government immediately collects **$1.80** out of the exchange.
- The Retailer is all excited about the vase, thinks it will sell quick so he displays it for sale for $25.00. Similar vases could go for at least twice as much. So it's a great deal!
- The customer comes into the store and realizes that the vase is exactly what will complete her living room. She must have it! She buys it for $25.00 plus $2.50 in sales tax for a total $27.50, still a bargain.
- The government immediately gets **$2.50** in tax from the store.
- Everyone is happy, no taxes to worry about, as they have been taken care of along the way, and the government has collected a total of **$6.70** in taxes for a $25.00 vase. Folks, that's **26%!!!** PAINLESS!
- **REMEMBER** – At the end of the year, the **Producer** does not have to report the silica sand sale, the **Manufacturer** does not have to declare the sale of the item it manufactured, the **Distributor** has nothing more to do about the vase sold to the retailer, and the **Retailer**, can continue to buy other great products. The **Customer**, now can enjoy that beautiful vase and the flowers and the joy that it brings to the household and not worry about filing taxes and hoping to get sufficient deductions by trying to get the best accountant possible to pay less to the government while hoping that on April 15 it does not rain or snow so they can all go out and have a picnic! That simple folks!

I know some of you are already saying that my TPPT will drive retail prices higher. Not so, because there is still the element of good old American rivalry in the marketplace. That will never change.

Although the value added taxes will have been taken care of, there is still the element of entrepreneurship. Some retailer would agree to only make, let's say 18% on any item, while others want to make 40%. Some will sell thousands of vases at $21.00 while others will sell hundreds at $25.00. That's the American way. Capitalism at work! Companies will find ways in which to sell their products at better rates than their competitors.

Ultimately, whether you buy a car, a surf board, a piece of clothing, a house, a bottle of booze or some kind of service, the "Painless Tax" is already added into the total of the purchase and gets automatically directed to the respective government coffers.

Each level of government takes their cut starting with local governments. The state government will use its share of the tax to fund schools, workman's compensation, Medicare, medical services for the uninsured, and all other items in the state budget. The remaining balance is then electronically sent to the Federal government to take care of things such as our social security, infrastructure, and the military industrial complex and to run our country and make improvements but stay out of the way of everything else. All this is accomplished and funded immediately, electronically and relatively painlessly.

And here is the best for last:

- In 2007 it was estimated by the Congressional Budget Office that there were $35 Trillion in national sales. That's our National Economy.
- Our yearly National Budget for 2012 is estimated to be $3.32 Trillion
- Based on the formula that I've listed, 26% in taxes is collected from any sold item (not included are services, food and beverages, etc.).
- This means that we would collect $7.5 to $9.0 Trillion in taxes each year.
- The end result is that we would be left with a bit over…are you ready for this: **$4.5 Trillion Dollars IN SURPLUS!**

No more April 15 tax filings, no more deductions, no more spending 37 cents out of every dollar you pay to the government to process your taxes (this has been the estimated costs to process your taxes, cited by a number of economic professors, economists and of course Republican politicians). No more "hidden" deductions or loopholes or smart attorneys to get a "deal" and no more corporate favoritism (i.e. General Electric, the biggest corporation in the world, getting away without paying any income taxes as they did in 2010).

There will be no more capital gain taxes, death taxes, inheritances or even lottery winning taxes. THE ONLY TAX YOU'LL PAY is when you buy something you can afford and it is "painless." That's it. No more!

And the best thing of all, you don't have to feel lousy about finding ways to pay the least amount of taxes or having to keep all those receipts to show how much you paid in retail taxes at the end of the year. Payments will all be done for you!

How you ask? Simple. We are going to get rid of our currency and all information will be recorded on your exclusive, totally unique, tamper-proof, National Identification Card. This card will store everything for you, including purchases, doctor's visits, medical history and all personal data. Only you can have access to it by using several protocols simultaneously, such as:

- Retinal recognition
- DNA verification
- Thumb imprint authentication
- And your own PIN or PASSWORD.

The National Identification Card will all be automatically updated and only you will have access to it or the person(s) you've assigned to take care of you.

No more having to keep tax records for at least seven to ten years, and no more sweating over how you are going to get sufficient money to pay property taxes, or those thousands of income tax dollars which are due April 15th.

In fact, April 15th should become a holiday to celebrate the National Day of Freedom!

In order to make this tax plan happen, there must also be a "Balanced Budget" amendment to our Constitution which prohibits every level of government from spending more than they take in. As an incentive to produce a balanced budget, every elected official will have his/her salary reduced by the percentage spent over the "Balanced Budget" they are responsible for overseeing.

How much do you want to bet me that we will have a balanced budget every year?

Spending what you can afford isn't such a novel idea, because most of us follow that principle (to live within our means), so why is it so strange for us to ask our government to abide by the same rules and save for a rainy day?

The reason it seems strange is because we are too lazy to hold public servants accountable. We let those whom we elect run wild while in office. We are more concerned about our favorite team's box scores, or whether Lindsey Lohan is going to jail or not, than what the government is doing with our money.

People we have to change that, NOW!

Of course it all goes back to my concept of "Term Limits." If a politician knows reelection is not a possibility and there is only so much time to put great ideas to work, they will do what is right. It's that simple folks: KISS!!!

CHAPTER 6

The Progressive Painless Tax
First, we must get rid of our currency!

Dollars were worth something around the world at one time. The global economy was (and still is) based on the value of the dollar and was the standard by which everything revolved in geo-global finances. But have you heard? The value of the dollar has begun shrinking because we keep printing more paper ever six months or so—bad idea.

Here's an example: What happens when your inventory is down to a few dozen gorgeous red roses and people must have them? You can basically charge what the market will bear; sometimes up to ten to twenty times their value.

Conversely, what happens when you have thousands of dozens of roses but only a few hundred people to buy? You've got to reduce their costs to sell them all. That's the same principle when traders buy and sell the dollar in the world-market; the more dollars that have been printed and in circulation, the lesser the value of each.

As a result, there is a good possibility that world economies will drop the dollar as their financial standard and switch to another currency because of the dollar's volatility and loss of value.

Then, what do you think is going to happen? I shudder to dwell too much on it because it would be terribly devastating for the economy. In fact, this decline has already started.

For the past two to three years, certainly from 2008 to the present, foreigners began flocking to our shores to buy our products because when they exchange their currency they get a lot more for their bang. For example, 10 English Pounds are now worth $15.87! The Brits are buying all they can handle.

Other currencies are alike until the dollar begins to gain strength.

Conversely, to buy something from another country, let's say Germany, Americans have to pay with more dollars than we used to. Our dollar does not carry as much weight any longer.

Before the collapse of the dollar takes place I have a shocking, far-fetched suggestion. Let's get rid of all our currency. Do away with dollar bills and coins and all that junk that we handle every day (*not really sanitary, by the way*), and replace it with our personal monetary card. Some already call it a "debit card" or ATM card, but let's call it the "Life" card.

Before we get too deep into the "Life" card, I'm suggesting changing to this personal card because one of the residual effects will be that EVERYONE WILL PAY THEIR FAIR SHARE OF TAXES. We've covered this a bit and we'll get into this later, but by using this single method of paying and thus collecting taxes from everyone, our deficit and our national tax collection will improve dramatically and we will not be able to print more dollars at a whim. Budgets will have to be balanced.

Besides in the history of the United States monetary record, we have started "from scratch" several times before, scraping our money and starting anew. Not impossible!

BACKGROUND:
- Almost every man, woman and child has or will have access to a wireless telephone.
- There are approximately 6.8 billion people on our planet. It was estimated in a study conducted by AT &T in 2009 that 5 billion will have a cell phone by the end of 2010, according to Lance Whitney, at TMCnet.com, technology journalist, web developer and software developer. That figure was met and surpassed.
- In 2008, a study indicated that over 75% of our day-to-day monetary transactions are done not with cash but with either a "debit" or "credit" card. Fast forward a few years and we may now be hovering around the

80%-plus mark of people using some type of card for all transactions.

- The elderly use debit cards less than most (53%), but perhaps that's because, they still have lots of cash hidden under their mattresses. Just kidding! Not really. Many of our elders were children or grandchildren of the Great Depression of 1929-1930, and knew first hand or heard of the stories told of individuals and families having lost all their currency overnight. Banks closed and with their closure went people's hard earned deposits. I'd be gun-shy as well to put all my money in banks.
- Americans are used to carrying less cash and making sure that there is sufficient money in their checking accounts to support their "debit card" spending. Credit cards may be used to buy larger items but because of the very negative news about people filing for bankruptcies and getting into deep credit problems, I believe most are trying to live within their means, thus the "Debit" card is our plastic cash.

Unlike my grandfather and my father, who used to walk around the house with pockets full of bills and coins to tempt the grand kids to chase him down, stick their hands in his pockets and see what they could get...times have changed. Those days are just a faint memory.

Today, when I occasionally take my grandkids shopping, all I do is carry the one card that I need for every transaction in the mall.

Checks are still OK to use, because in some cases you can "float" the money by maybe one or two days or more. (Float -- That's the time it takes from when you first hand a check over the counter until it actually hits your bank and is deducted from your account.)

However some stores, especially the larger ones have gotten really smart and they do not delay deposits anymore. Instead, certain stores accept your check and immediately run it through their system which logs into your bank to take the funds out instantly. So that two to three-day "float" of your money doesn't work anymore.

- Almost 84% of all licensed businesses in the United States process credit cards for their transactions, according to a 2010 National Association of Better Business survey. It's estimated that figure is almost 95% in 2012; especially with the advent of a number of machines and telephones that make it easier and cheaper to accept credit/debit card transactions.
- The exceptions, of course, are when you go to a garage sale and pick up a book for fifty-cents or a chair for $10.00, or you go to the grocery store for a loaf of bread or a can of tomato sauce; if it's less than ten dollars, often consumers pay with cash.
- But that habit of quick transactions will have to be changed to implement what I'm suggesting. (Wait until you hear what the change will mean and the positive effects it will have on our society.)

By the way our society is already changing the way it handles money and personal communication. Therefore, the suggestions to get rid of all cash transactions may not be as ridiculous as some may think.

SOLUTION: Since folks are already accustomed to "money cards," a "Life" card is an easy sell. This card will be issued to every person in this country (and perhaps in the world, in time).

In our case, the card might also contain encrypted personal data accessible by the owner through a series of identifying methods including: retinal, DNA-sensitive, thumbprint and unique password identification, all accepted simultaneously.

The "Life" card would have the following embedded information (with the potential of containing other data as required):

- Name
- Date of birth
- Gender
- Address
- Parent information (for children under eighteen)
- Social Security number
- Citizenship
- Bank(s) account
- Record of earnings
- Current bank account balances
- Medical records
- Record of transaction(s)
- Taxes paid year-to-date

- And much more if you wish

IMPORTANT FACTS TO KNOW:

- The "Life" card must be tamper-proof. We have the technology for that right now! Encryption can only be accessed by the owner and cannot be accessed or used by anyone else; even the wife, husband, parent, brother, sister, close friend etc., without certain protocols being set up in advance. In the case of a child, the parent can take the child or card to their local "Life" card bank and make necessary changes.
- If the card is lost, it cannot be used by anyone else. It can only be used by the proper bearer because of the redundant procedures to use it, such as: Retinal, DNA, thumbprint and password protections. You must have all four to access the card.
- As stated above, "Life" cards cannot be duplicated, but can be replaced with a totally encrypted new code that only the owner can have originated.
- Are these cards possible? Yes, absolutely. Let me tell you that the technology is already there and being used today in various forms.
- In some businesses, for example, you need your retinal identification plus your thumb or hand print to access certain departments. You cannot enter a building without it. This is especially so in government offices, NASA and DuPont, Facebook, Google, and many other high-security businesses. We are already used to having to use passwords to access almost everything we deal through the day. And

DNA technology is already being used in medical centers, doctor's offices and the military.

- Therefore, blowing air through your mouth into a special chip on the "Life" card is easy enough. The chip accepts your DNA and for the next thirty-seconds, that card is "live." So combining all these into a single "Life" card is absolutely possible, doable and makes a lot of sense. The technology is here ready to be used.

- WHAT IF SOMEONE DIES? – Good question. Once a person dies, the card can be taken to a local bank or ID center to have all the information purged, recorded, transferred to the person or persons or entities delineated in the card, and eventually all the information in the card is totally eliminated from the system. This is not unlike what survivors have to do now, except that most if not all of the personal information of a person is on one "Life" card. Can you imagine not having to call the Social Security Administration, closing all the accounts a person incurs during a life time, employer(s), department stores, utilities, etc. For most people it is a one to two-week process, I know it was for me when my mother and father passed away. With the "Life" card it is all taken care of in one stop. Amazing!

- If a card is lost by a competent person, the owner can just stop by one of the thousands of "Life" card centers and get a new one. Again, you don't have to spend hours upon hours calling everyone when you lose your wallet or purse.

- If the card is lost by an elder or a child or someone who has lost competency a parent or guardian would go into a "Life" card office and reconstruct the entire card.
- Parents, husbands or wives and significant others can be placed on file in the event the person dies or is incapable of acting on his/her own behalf, to make changes or access bank accounts. Most of us do that right now with our off-springs or survivors.

Of course there are many, many scenarios that can be brought up where steps must be taken to prevent someone from taking advantage of another person, such a divorced couples, trying to tap on the ex's account, contracts, wills, etc. Once the premise of this "Life" card is accepted then we can work out these "details."

WHAT ARE THE BENEFITS OF THE "LIFE" CARD?
Hold on to your hats because there are many and they are all good:

1. You and only you own your identity and no one else.
2. The government or anyone else cannot access your card without proper identification or permission or some type of court order.
3. The card can only be used by you after you've gone through the protocol.
4. What is the protocol? Before any transaction, you hold the "Life" card close to your eye for five seconds, then, breath onto the chip on your card, and then proceed to put your thumb on the exact location

indicated on the card before you swipe it. Once swiped, you'll be asked for your own code or password. You'll have sufficient time to do this. Try it. Grab one of your cards, hold it close to your eye, blow into it, place your thumb on a portion and then swipe it. It should take you less than five to ten seconds to do it.

5. Failure to meet all these requirements and positively identify each, will abort any transaction.

6. With the "Life" card every aspect of your life can be recorded if you so choose and released only upon your request or by order of the court.

7. Remember, only the owner will set up what he or she wants in that card. The storage of such information is not available to anyone else, including the government, unless, access is gained through the courts or through special circumstances.

8. On the practical side, you will not need to fill out endless forms for a job, for the doctor, or even when applying for a loan, etc. All that information will be stored in a personal data master file center(s). And only you can release exactly what you want through a menu pop-up by which you choose what information is released and when.

9. These massive personal data centers will be located throughout the United States with back-ups in several friendly countries. Data will ultimately be stored in a number of satellites in space; all wirelessly interconnected and changing simultaneously with upgrades, balances and other updates. This will be a

fool-proof, back-up system of unprecedented proportions.

Note: As it often happens nowadays just when you think you've thought of everything, new ideas appear in an instant. Such is the case of the "Life Card." I wrote this portion of the book sometime in mid-2010. Two years later, just speaking with people, including my young and very alert grandkids, I found out that it is now possible to have a "chip" on your finger tip that will access all the information contained in the "Life Card" at an instant. It is possible one day, all we will have to do is swipe our finger or our hand over a "computer reader" and access any record that we own and conclude a transaction.

These young wipper-snappers tell me that it is now possible. Who would have thunk it?

NOW FOR THE PURPOSES OF COLLECTING TAXES:

When purchasing a product or service with the card, at the moment of your transaction, all sales information will be instantly recorded on your personal "Life" card. This will include the amount of tax you've paid. All transactions, no matter how big or how small, will be recorded and the tax you've paid will be credited to your "Life" card account.

You will know exactly how much tax you have paid at any time during the year. It will also show how that tax was distributed to include: taxes sent to your local township, city, county, state and the federal government. All this will take place at the moment of your transaction. You will control every operation and not depend on a business to distribute the taxes accordingly.

Remember, this is the only time you will have to deal with any taxes, because there are no other forms to complete or deadlines to meet. Taxes in the manner we've been used to, will disappear for EVERYONE!

Some people say that the very poor should not have to pay any taxes. I agree. We must help. So here is something that will take place effortlessly, seamlessly and automatically, once everyone has the "Life" card.

Taxes will be assessed according to your earnings level indicated in your previous year's earnings records. Based upon that number, you may or may not get a refund on the TPPT money you've paid during the current year. The calculations to see whether you get money back or not will be automatically computed twice a year: June 30th and December 31st.

This process will quell the argument that it is unfair for poor people to pay the same percentage that rich people pay. In most cases, people below the poverty level will not pay any taxes at all.

The "Poverty Level" figure will be determined by Congress, which by the way, would know better than most what it should be since Congress is responsible for many families falling into poverty in the first place.

The absolute fairness of this system really shows when someone of wealth purchases a high-dollar item. Since the "Life" card tracks every single transaction including when you get paid and when you pay someone else, it will be easy to determine income, spending and tax levels.

For example, the person who just bought a 45 million-, dollar Citation Jet will pay the tax installment of "**The Progressive Painless Tax.**" Remember, taxes have already been collected from the moment that Citation became a concept on the drawing board and all the way through its manufacture and eventual sale. The system is simple and fair because folks are taxed only on what they choose to spend.

Here are more benefits that I believe make this structure all the more worthwhile. Please remember that we are abolishing all currency and for all intents and purposes, currency and coins will disappear from our economy as everything is run through the "Life" card:

1. Only legal citizens can obtain the "Life" card for use.
2. Temporary visitors residing in the United States will get the "T-Life" card and pay the same as everyone else; but only for the time they have a Visa to be in the United States. They can stop by with their passport and visa at any "Life" card center have one issued.
3. Illegal residents in the United States need not fear. They will have their own "I-Life" card, but will pay an additional TPPT percentage and an additional "foreign resident" tax to discourage them from illegally entering this country.

EDITOR'S NOTE: We have an entire chapter on the illegal situation in the United States and how to resolve it. Many of the questions herein will be answered.

Published reports indicate that 8% to 9% of our yearly sales, which were around 14 trillion dollars in 2010, exchanged hands in this underground economy. This covers cash payments to baby sitters, handymen and women, gardeners, crop pickers, illegals, other manual laborers, and even the uniquely American exchange known as the "garage sale."

The biggest positive outcome of the "Life," the "T-Life" and "I-Life" cards includes the ability to track the purchase of everything obtained in this country, BY THE INDIVIDUAL WHO MADE THE PURCHASES.

The system will at the very least, collect taxes on illegal transactions, even though the parties to the transaction may NOT be tracked. If they buy something in the United States, they MUST have some type of an account that will be activated with one of the "Life" cards. This is because there is no currency!

Moreover, we already have limits on currency going out and coming into the United States. Smuggling would only be the possible way to move great quantities of foreign cash. We have preventive measures for that too, albeit they are not full-proof.

Drug dealers sell drugs to make money so that they can buy great houses, fine clothes, lots of cars and women...mostly. But if there are NO CASH transactions what will they use for money?

The "Life" card will record all transactions. Do you think they want the government to know what their business is? But even if they figure out how to bypass the new monetary system, work around it, or shade it under a bogus company;

taxes will nonetheless be collected for every transaction because eventually the money they have must be laundered into the monetary system. How great is that? Taxation without representation for the crooks!

(Before you think we are letting drug dealers off the hook, look to Chapter 13 for a solution to our drug problem.)

There is at least one more benefit. Counterfeiting will be finished forever! Copying and printing any denomination won't do anyone a bit of good. Cash will be worthless. Have at it boys and gals!

You think that the same counterfeiters will then switch to counterfeit "Life" cards? I doubt it. These bio-metric, impossible to duplicate cards cannot be copied by anyone as long as part of the process includes the personal "touch" of the rightful owner. Do you really think that someone can duplicate your breath and the DNA contents therein? Do you really think that someone can duplicate your own retinal dynamics? Just those two elements alone will make the "Life" card bulletproof. And, as noted earlier, once all that information is stored in your finger, finger tips or hand, Poof! It's over!

We have the technology today to make the "Life" card tamper-proof. Some people will say that it is just a dream. Not so, the technology exists today to make this card. In fact, it is already being applied in various forms. It just needs to be integrated. IT CAN BE DONE!

Is there the potential that technology will change and the cards may be compromised; either through illegal internal recordkeeping or access to the master files, or through other forms of corruption? Possibly.

But at some point we must rely on our government and the specialists who work for us to set up barriers, stop-gaps and other security measures for the entire system.

And yes, once the world adapts these systems, we'll have people outside the United States trying to beat the process. We just have to be smarter than they are by inserting insurmountable barriers at every turn.

Is this wishful thinking? Perhaps. But what we have now is certainly not even close to being better.

THE PRACTICALLITY OF A "LIFE" CARD:

- Let's say that you wish to pay your rent. The landlord has an account into which you can deposit your $500.00 either at the bank or online or by swiping his/her "reader." In either case, the 10% TPPT tax will be collected from the landlord. So your total payment of $500.00 will automatically be deducted from your account and into the Landlord's account. However, immediately thereafter $50 will be taken out of his account and credited for tax and showing that he has paid the tax. Your landlord does not have to report that income. Remember, there are no taxes to file. It was done in an instant. Painless!

- Perhaps you wish to purchase a lovely dress from your neighbor and she wants $30.00 for it. She does not have a business license or a shop. So she whips out her cell phone and if it does not have it already, she plugs in a port to read "debit" cards or "credit" cards. Before handing you her cell phone to swipe your card, she has set it up so that the amount you are paying for the dress goes directly to her account. She keys-in $30.00. Before swiping the card, you have the card recognize your retina and DNA then place your thumb over the reader on the card and key-in your "code." Immediately, your account is charged $30.00 (with the 10% TPPT tax sent). $27.00 goes to the seller's account and $3.00 to the tax account in one of the thousands of centers in the U.S. where it gets distributed through the banking system and into township/city, county, state and federal government reserve accounts. That's it! Done!

Neither person needs to account for the transaction or tax payment because it's already done for you. There is no requirement for you to do any reporting. The seller does not have to report their income or tax liability either as it is all done progressively and automatically. You have done your duty, contributed to our society and can just go on.

No more April 15th, or forms to fill out, no more accountants, no more layers, no more deductions and loopholes, no more paying for workman's compensation, FICA, SDI, Social Security, et. al. Everything is included in that transaction, everything!

Tell me that this is not the best thing you've ever heard of? Besides, what we have now is hardly up to par.

Important disclaimer here: For the purposes of this book and this chapter, I've applied a formula based upon a 10% tax.

However, I would leave the determination of the exact percentage of tax revenue to run every level of this country, up to much smarter people.

Keep in mind that in addition to not having to file income taxes, state taxes, etc., there will be no inheritance taxes, no death taxes or no gift taxes. There will be only ONE tax that will fund all levels of government, **THE PROGRESSIVE PAINLESS TAX!**"

CHAPTER 7

National Debt -
(Don't buy what you can't afford!)

This is a short chapter because there really isn't much that can be stated except the obvious: **DO NOT SPEND MORE MONEY THAN YOU COLLECT!**

This is such a simple concept; yet, our government does not adhere to the practicality of it.

My wife, children and even my grandchildren understand the concept of not spending what you don't have. Most of us do and live by it. We can't spend more than what we have in our checking account or in the box under our bed. If we do, we are in serious trouble. Especially if we use credit cards, which more often than not go delinquent and the percentage of interest sky-rockets to beyond "usury" levels.

It is so basic to live within your means; yet our Federal government continues not to understand the concept and persists to spend like drunken sailors. I blame them because they have gotten used to spending more than we have in our coffers or hope to have. And why not?

Have we not also read that in many cases the House Bank reports a plethora of members of Congress showing overdrawn bank accounts? According to an article in Wikipedia, 22 members of Congress have overdrawn or abused their bank accounts. Here's what was reported:

"The House Bank functioned according to rules different from the laws governing deposit institutions. The facility was operated under very loose rules at the time, using a pencil and ledger system rather than a computerized accounting system, and the bank manager did not provide regular account statements to House members, nor were notifications sent to House members in the event they had overdrawn their accounts. Further contributing to the problem was the fact that the House Bank didn't post deposits in a timely manner, often as much as seven weeks after the fact. Thus, while some knowingly took advantage of the system (and were ultimately convicted of wrongdoing) many members of the House who wrote overdrafts were not actually at fault, as it was the House Bank's responsibility to post deposits in a timely manner.

Another practice which contributed to the scandal was that House members were allowed to overdraw their accounts, provided that the overdraft did not exceed the member's next paycheck. Many House members used this practice to take unauthorized advances on their paychecks which they would repay in the future. In a corporate context the practice of drawing money out of the corporation's accounts for personal use is a violation of fiduciary duty to the corporation's shareholders. Many U.S. banks, like the House Bank, offered overdraft protection to checking account holders."

So when you have people used to abusing or taking advantage of their banking privileges is it so shocking that Congress has amended our laws to raise the "debt ceiling" or continuously printed more money to increase our spending budgets and our debt limits? They see this as part of doing business as usual!

We have reached the boiling point. "Debt-Armageddon" is here! No more counting on the tax payer for more money to spend. All recent Presidents have been at fault, but our present Administration has taken spending to absolutely unheard of new levels while creating indebtedness beyond anyone's imagination.

They are collecting a bit over four trillion dollars and spending over thirteen trillion. That increase is ten times larger than any president going back even to Jimmy Carter's Administration. Why?

Really simple: President Barak Obama was elected by a majority who were looking for a government handout either for themselves or for others. Not all of them were poor, disenfranchised and below the poverty level, mind you. Many were the richest most affluent people in our country.

These people use everyone else's money to make themselves even richer beyond comprehension, as evidenced by the Goldman Sack debacle of a few years ago and Freddy Mack and Fanny Mae; all controlled by the wealthy under the watchful eye of our so-called government.

Democrats insisted on making loans even to those who could not afford them just to gain popularity for future elections, while Republicans took the opportunity to make even more money.

Can you blame them? Of course not. That's why many people go into business, to take every advantage available for them to succeed and make a better life for themselves.

However, you CAN blame those politicos who support and allow liberal business practices and tax loopholes for the rich to take advantage of by stretching the law, circumventing checks and balances and making it practically impossible for the average citizen to challenge. Blame those politicians who prey on some to meet the needs of others for the sake of being elected and reelected *(See Chapter 1 for a cure to that problem)*.

SOLUTION: Change the Constitution so that there is a Balanced Budget Amendment and add the Line Item Veto to make sure nothing is questionably inserted in the creation of a new law or amending one.

Politicians often add their pet legislation to a popular bill surreptitiously; knowing full well that if that item was on its own as a possible law, it would never pass. This is done by design.

In other words, a conversation between lawmakers could go something like this: *"I'll help you pass your proposed law if we insert my pet law into it."* With the line-item option, none of the so-called "pet-legislation" could get through or be allowed. Each new law would stand on its own merits.

Moreover, we must pass a law that says if anyone from the President of the United States on down to governors and mayors, allows an overrun of the budget; they should be impeached.

It's that simple folks. The people want fiduciary responsibility from our elected officials.

Democrats and Republicans continue to claim that a balance budget amendment is simply not the answer. Bull, I say!

I'm a Republican in spirit, but more than that, I'm an American who wants to have the best for my family, friends and the people of this great country of ours. I say, damn the fracturing effects of Republican, Democrat, Libertarian, or any party centered agenda.

DO WHAT IT IS RIGHT FOR THE PEOPLE and I'll have your back. Fail to enact laws consistent with our Constitution and for the good of the people and I'll be your worst nightmare!

CHAPTER 8

Who can vote?
Not you if...!

I can't believe that we test everyone for proficiency in the most mundane of things but fail to assess their preparedness to vote in local, state and federal elections. The Constitution gives the voting rights to all citizens of the United States. Unfortunately, many who probably don't even know how to spell "Constitution," also have that right.

How can we elect people who will serve us well when many voters do not take the time to learn about the candidate by studying his/her background? Even worse, many voters have no concept or even an inkling as to what governance is all about. They have no idea what they should expect of a candidate.

I'd say that if a citizen can't answer a few questions particular to our current government, they should not receive a license to vote. Yes, I said "license" to vote. That's simple. (Certain to be challenged by the ACLU and a multitude of liberties watch dogs.)

Certain folks may say that this idea is heartless, prejudicial, bigoted, discriminating, and wrong. It is NOT wrong.

Certainly each citizen's unalienable right to vote should not be revoked, but we should impose laws so that when you use your right you do it with some modicum of knowledge and experience.

This principle can be illumined by the following examples: A young child has the freedom to swim, but unless he/she knows how, it is not prudent to drop him/her into the surf out at sea. Likewise, folks have the freedom to eat, but consider the outcome if they didn't know which foods were safe to consume.

It is with these examples in mind that I suggest that every citizen of the United States may exercise their right to vote only after he/she has passed a basic test to demonstrate an ability to make an educated vote.

Allow me to explain how I see this exercise being accomplished when it comes to elections…

LOCAL, STATE & NATIONAL ELECTIONS: Prior to voting, every citizen should answer a few simple questions which relate to the vote at hand. Taking a test and answering maybe 8 out of the 15 questions correctly would be sufficient to allow the voter to cast his/her vote. Questions might include:

- Who is the current mayor of your city or town?

- Name at least three (3) people who sit on the current City Council.
- Give the name of the current municipal Chief of Police.
- Give the name of the current local Fire Chief.
- List the name of the current Superintendent of Schools for the district you live in.
- Who is the principle of the high school nearest to you?
- Who is the President of the United States?
- Who is the Vice-President of the United States?
- Name one of the two U.S. Senators from your state.
- Who is the congressional representative for your district?
- In what district do you reside?
- Who is your state representative?
- When was the Declaration of Independence of the United States written?
- Who was the first President of the United States?
- Was Abraham Lincoln ever President of the United States? And if so, what was his name? *(Just being silly.)*

Of course these questions can be fine-tuned. It seems that if a basic competency were established with at least six or eight of the above questions, we could certify an individual is qualified to use his/her "unalienable" right to vote. A voting card for that date would verify voting eligibility for those who meet testing requirements before every vote on a local, state or federal level.

Is there something wrong with that? I don't think so. I don't think being required to establish that you know what you are doing infringes on your rights.

Just like you can't drive without a license; you can't get legally married without a license; you can't provide professional public help without a license; you can't vote without a certificate! Otherwise, why don't we let children vote as well? I have four grandchildren that have better overall political knowledge than most college kids.

You think I'm kidding about some college students not being competent to vote? Just watch some of the nightly Jay Leno Shows. I'm referring to the segments that feature Jay on the streets asking simple questions of people he encounters on a random basis (of course, I know that the show is edited and slanted to make people look foolish and pass it on as entertainment), but watching these segments is really scary. To think these might be the leaders in the future!

I cringe every time I see the folks he encounters. I agonize because I realize that some of these youngsters, in particular, will never get a break in life. The uneducated will suffer until the day they die because they have no clue.

As I said before, it's likely that Leno likes to feature those who do not know the answers to the basic political questions, I'm almost sure of that. Hopefully, there are as many or more interviewed who know the answers to all of his questions. Unfortunately, featuring competent citizens doesn't make good television – at least according to these producers.

Even if it just a few who are clueless as to what goes on round the world, that's enough to push the "panic" button.

Do I want one these people changing my diapers at my old age? Do I want one of them picking up my trash, while driving a 10-ton truck around? I don't think so. Nor do I want some of them filling my prescription, giving me a DMV driving test or answering questions about my social security benefits. And certainly I don't want any of them voting towards my future and that of others.

Of course many politicians count on getting votes from people such as these, who are easily swayed by the fact that the politician promises to help them get their piece of the pie. These are people who are waiting to be led, but where? That's another story.

But even uneducated votes count and that's how some politicians, even some presidents get elected. Don't you agree? If you do, isn't that sad, criminally apathetic, and patently wrong?

How can we hope to continue to improve ourselves, set standards for the world through our actions and carry on to profess the solid belief that our democracy works, unless we have educated people who not only make an educated vote but can stand to influence others through their daily lives? You can't have one without the other.

CHAPTER 9

Illegal Immigration –
How to do away with it.

PROBLEM: Illegal immigration.
SOLUTION: Simple. Shoot them all!
Simple enough?

Of course I'm being facetious and silly, but there is a solution to the problem.

This country, in its short life span of three-hundred-plus years, was built on the promise of allowing people to come to our shores, work the land and reap its benefits. The United States was built by people who sought freedom and the right to fend for themselves. They found these privileges here.

It was and is a great concept. Millions still clamor to come to the United States, the land of opportunity -- like no other.

Most want to take a chance, work the land and explore the possibilities that only this country really offers. The United States offers people the chance to make something of themselves.

We know that there are very few countries that extend such an opportunity. So why blame those who want to come to America, whether legally or illegally? We must realize that this carrot is too sweet to not pursue.

Of course some immigrants just want to come to the United States to take advantage of the very liberal benefits we offer without putting much effort into finding a job or working for their own sustenance. These people tax our principles, kill our economy and test our resolution to continue accepting newcomers to our nation.

Being a "legal" immigrant myself, I know the feeling of coming to the brave new world of America. When my mother, my sister and I crossed under the Golden Gate Bridge on a cargo ship back in the early fifty's, we thought that heaven was waiting with doors wide open to us. My father had arrived months earlier, and after waiting for five years to get a visa for us, greeted us on the dock with an exuberant anticipation that I had never seen in his face before.

We settled in Los Angeles. Mom began working, dad worked two jobs and my sister and I went to school. We melded very well into the community and contributed to the society without being a burden to anyone else. Millions like us have done the same thing.

While many immigrants come to this nation to enrich and contribute to our communities, just as many are not really pulling their weight. The United States is spending billions of dollars to take care of their needs; including providing for their children, as well as family health, education and everything else a normal life requires.

We do so because we are the United States. A country that has taken in the very poor, the uneducated, the slave and the downtrodden and provided opportunity for the person who is willing to search and work for an improved life. In those days, we didn't just hand out gifts, but invited people to come to our shores, show initiative and God willing, to make something better of life.

But now we are going broke. We can no longer sustain what we have done. Something has to change.

We Americans have not become heartless, selfish, or self-consumed overnight. Fortunately, our hearts remain as gentle and caring as they have ever been. We understand the struggles that people go through and why they come here. We can imagine the conditions and the setbacks people suffer in oppressive societies. As neighbors, we feel for them because most realize that only a select few can make it in their country

Therefore, I propose that the United States:
- Take care of every illegal person asking for help without turning anyone down and that we provide anything that they want including: housing, transportation, clothing, etc.
- Provide for their education.
- Arrange for their healthcare.

- Give them free medicine.
- Give them a welfare check every month they have qualified.

We MUST take care of them!

No, I'm not going crazy. Read on...

HOW TO DO IT?

Pass legislation that will support what I'm about to outline and these related caveats.

- Add up the daily cost of providing for each **illegal immigrant.** Include taxes and everything else that all **legal** citizens have to pay as well.
- Immediately after providing them with service, bill the amount on a per-person and per-occasion basis to the **Country of Their Origin (COTO)**!

- Say what? Too simple?

- Yes, it's the "**COTO**" principle!
- Payments from each Country of Origin might initially be collected by partially freezing each country's deposits in the U.S. to take care of their citizens' bills.
- If there aren't sufficient funds to get paid for services rendered, the next step is to tag that amount to the trade debt we might have against each country.
- If we don't owe them anything, add that amount to their next trade exchange with us.

- If that doesn't work, cut that portion of our annual "Foreign Aid" to each country by the amount they owe us.
- If there are no funds, tap their account at the World Bank.
- As a worst case scenario, put a lien on each country who owes a debt to us.

I love it! Mexico, if they cannot pay their bills, could be ours in let's say, ten or fifteen years!

In actuality, this would never happen because as soon as Mexico (and other countries), realize that their citizens are running up a bill with us, those borders will be shut down faster than an old maid's door.

We can still continue to be the temperate people we were known to be and for the most part still are, while holding someone accountable to finally pay for the goods we provide to illegal immigrants.

At this point, it looks like Mexico would be the country most indebted to us. According to the U.S. Department of Homeland Security, the countries of origin with the largest numbers of illegal immigrants are as follows (latest as of 2009):

1. México -   62%
2. El Salvador -   5%
3. Guatemala -   4%
4. Honduras -   3%
5. Philippines -   2%
6. India -   2%

7. Korea -   2%
8. Other countries -   20%

If we were to change our system and begin to bill the **COTO**, here are some general calculations of the costs that our neighbors to the south would have to bear for services rendered in the United States to illegal Mexican Nationals and their children:

- $18,000,000.00 <u>per day</u> for schooling, health care, medicine, Medicaid, and welfare or supplemental income for families with children; among a number of other benefits.
- In one week, that amount would increase to approximately $126,000,000.00.
- Taking it further, in one year, Mexico would owe the United States approximately 6.6 billion dollars plus interest and mounting!

Implementing **COTO** allows us to welcome immigrants while recuperating our costs.

To service our business needs here in the U.S., why not set up a Working Foreign Visa (WFV) program so that we can ask for help when needed. Workers can come into the U.S. to work, pay taxes and pay for their own sustenance.

Wherever a guest under the WFV program lives or works, he/she must show their WFV ID and then is issued an I-Life Card. When the WFV expires; they must return to their homeland or join the rolls of those illegals that are costing their country of origin *"muchos pesos."* Mexico will make sure they are sent back, I can almost guarantee you that.

Who wants to bet that under the **COTO** principle, Mexico and other countries, would close their borders tighter than size 6 shoes, on Michael Jordan?

Can you see this simple-minded solution to a problem that has haunted us for generations, as brilliant? Well, maybe not brilliant but pretty good, I would say.

Our borders will finally be sealed as other nations restrict illegal emigration, thereby allowing only those who want to come into the United States through legal processes to leave their homeland.

I'd bet that Mexico would be the first to stand on their side of the border, ready to stop anyone from trying to get into the U.S.

Problem solved.
Next...

CHAPTER 10

- National Healthcare -
Who gets it and who does not?

Is it heartless for me to say, "Why should I worry about your healthcare, while I have my own and my family's care to worry about?"

Of course I realize that not everyone is as lucky as I am. There are people who really don't have any support base (i.e. family, friends, pension, health insurance, rich uncles, etc.) to take up the cause.

Healthcare, like abortion is an issue that I don't believe will ever be narrowed to a clear-cut, decisive answer that will satisfy everyone in this country. So what's the simple solution, to this great dilemma?

TAKE STEPS TO AVOID GETTING SICK!

As asinine and basic as that sounds, we can go a long way towards preventing illness, even in our old age.

Not getting sick means living a clean life; including exercising on a regular basis, and eating a diversity of foods in moderate portions on defined schedules while alternating food choices to bring about a balanced diet. Of course, one should not eat or drink alcohol to excess or smoke at all.

I believe your body was set up to go on until a pre-determined time before you were born. If you believe in God, he probably said, "Let's see, will give Elias 86 years to live, starting on January 1942 and ending the winter of 2028.

On the other hand, for those of you who don't believe in God, then it's your job not to get run over by a car or drop out of the sky in an airplane.

I figure that if I live a balanced life, in 2028 they'll be celebrating at my wake to the good life that I led.

Unfortunately, many of us don't know how to live a "balanced" life. We begin to kill ourselves from the moment we begin to make decisions. Some people think that they will live forever and could care less whether they overeat or drink to excess on a regular basis. Others don't give a shit because life is short and they figure they might as well enjoy it while they can. Slice me into this category. And still others blame everyone else for their illness and subsequent demise.

So why are we trying to find an answer? It's the human thing to do. It's the right thing to do. It's the American thing to do; even though ironically, when it comes to our own body, some of us forget the issue.

THE PROBLEM:

Our socio/economic standards of living have divided our nation. Our current president is attempting to divide us even further. Yes, the rich, the middle class and the poor have to contend with the same illnesses and setbacks. Unfortunately:

1. Not everyone enjoys or can afford a good health care program during their lifetime.
2. Many don't have family members or caregivers to assist them when they become ill.
3. Some can't get the right treatment where they live, so they are stuck with what's available.

Where I live, there's minimal health support. We are in a small town in the middle of the desert and the nearest full-care facility is at least 45 miles away. I am fortunate that I have transportation that I can drive those forty to sixty miles to get to a good health care provider. But there are thousands of people who do not have transportation and have to rely on friends or public transportation to get them out. More often than not they are stuck.

SOLUTION:
1. Allow every single authorized insurance company to sell their insurance package or coverage in all 50th States and Territories of the United States.

Competition will yield better coverage at a lesser rate. Currently, this is not possible as insurance companies are mandated as to where they can or cannot sell their product by the Federal and State governments.

2. Develop a formula for every insurance company in the United States to contribute to a "special" fund, based upon the net gross by each carrier, for those who can't afford to buy insurance.

3. Call the new insurer the "United States Health Care" company.

4. Change the law by initiating the "Tort Reform" suggested in a previous chapter. If applied, insurance companies will not be as exposed to catastrophic awards; therefore they will be able to tailor packages according to individuals' need. Lower litigation costs will free them from having to get the most out of every policyholder to guard against major losses.

5. Establish time limits as to when claims can be filed; usually, within a year of the accident.

6. Underwrite the staffing for the United States Health Care Company's coverage with the funds contributed by each insurance company according to a percentage of support.

7. Do not let the government or any arm thereof, closer than one hundred miles from getting involved in this USHC program. In other words, the Government MUST NOT run this program.

8. Insurance companies who participate in USHC will select a board comprised of citizens, including attorneys, doctors and health care administrators to manage the program.

9. Those receiving FREE health care must meet the required criterion. Those receiving care must be below the poverty level, out of work, or currently unable to pay for health care because of other conditions. Each person or family under this program will be audited yearly for compliance.

10. People committing fraud in the program will be prosecuted to the fullest extent of the law.

11. Remember that our famous "Life Card" will have all that information first-hand, including financial conditions. In addition, since we would have abolished all types of currency, the "Life Card" will be able to provide such information (if the individual feels it necessary or forfeit insurability), that is absolutely accurate.

12. Provide the either/or "option" to everyone working to establish a mandatory "Health Care Savings/Investment Account" by allowing each person to choose a money manager vetted by a consortium of advocates.

13. Cleaning our Drug and Alcohol programs. (*You'll love the idea and you will know where most of the funding for this is obtained. Read Chapter 13.*)

Done deal!

WAIT, SOMETHING JUST HAPPENED...

Deal not yet done! As we were going through our second and final editing proof of this book, the Obama Care health coverage package (6/29/12) was ruled constitutional by the High Court and by Chief Justice Roberts' vote (five to four in favor), saying that it was a "tax" mandate not a "penalty," thus opening the door for the opposition (Republicans and Tea Party, and others), to pounce on President Obama for going against what he promised during his first three years; basically when he said, "That there would be no new taxes with the Health Care program."

Oh, yeah? This could be tantamount to the famous ditty by President Bush (41st), who said: *"Read my lips, no new taxes."* And of course we know what happened to George Herbert Bush, it cost him his reelection.

CHAPTER 11

Cheap Oil & New Energy

PROBLEM: We need oil, and lots of it, because most of our infrastructure depends on petroleum and oil-based products.

SOLUTION: Change our infrastructure so that it runs on alternative resources like: solar, wind, clean coal, water, air, steam, soy beans, corn, atoms, and even cooking oil. We have the technology already, so what's the holdup?

HOLDUP: Powerful lobbies (see Chapter 1), powerful corporations, and powerful elected officials who can ramrod just about any legislation they want, as long as someone puts money into their reelection coffers (see Chapter 1 again).

BACKGROUND: According to the CATO Institute, we send $800 billion U.S. dollars just to the Middle East every year to pay for the oil we consume. We spend over a trillion dollars with all other countries. That figure includes transportation, insurance, processing, etc., which in some cases goes to a third party. Nevertheless, 800 billion is a lot of change that could enrich our economy if we kept it here.

I saw a video that really puts this figure into the right perspective. The producers noted that if you could spend a million dollars a day from the date that Jesus Christ was born until today, you would have spent a lot less than $800 billion. Forget about lining up dollar bills next to each other to see how far 800 billion-dollars-worth would go. It would stretch into the next galaxy, I suppose.

It is ridiculous that we spend that much money on foreign oil and do it so willingly. Why?

Some say we should distribute the wealth and keep half of the world solvent, thus eliminating the possibilities of wars. Hello?

What has happened in the Middle East in the last fifty years, the last twenty years, even in the last five years?

Multiple wars -- that's what, and mostly to protect our oil interests. Although some would argue that we are bringing democratic values to the world.

Nonetheless, in the process we have made a select few richer than anyone could have ever imagined. The irony of all ironies is that a few of these very rich "nomads," actually fund others to take our country down and destroy our way of life. Are we stupid? Are we insane? Are we several cards short off a full deck for allowing these clowns to take us down that path?

This idiocy must stop! Of course some will say that we cannot produce sufficient oil to take care of our needs. I say bunk! Diddle Squat! Bull-pucky!

We have plenty of resources including the outer shale gas, natural gas, clean coal, and recently tapped coal bed methane, oil and natural gas deposits located in sedimentary rocks. We have more than enough assets to pump it from our fields and seas and bring back those billions of dollars where they belong; to the United States.

Screw those tattered craniums. I'm trying to be politically correct here, but they are your basic oil parasites of the world.

However, working against this is the bigger problem that our economy heavily depends on oil. There are several factions who claim that we have an environmental duty to save this nation and urge us to drill somewhere else and not contaminate ourselves here in the U.S.

Even so, I believe that the United States could close all ties with other countries today and begin to tap our own oil at a much cheaper rate. However, I suspect that some people in the inner circles of Washington, D. C., might argue that we should use up international oil before we tap into our own supply. This logic is a stretch, but I would not put it past them to apply it successfully.

Nonetheless, even if that were to be true, we are still sending outrageous amounts of money that could be kept here to make this country whole again. I'm more concerned about the welfare of our nation than arguments about the environment or oil reserves. So I think that kind of thinking is absolute nonsense.

We have new environmentally friendly drilling methods that can be as efficient as 99%, according to Bonner R. Cohen, Adjunct Fellow with the National Center for Public Policy Research, a think-tank in Washington, D.C. According to Mr. Cohen, the only species to be affected by drilling in the Arctic National Wildlife Refuge (ANWR) is the canard. "Canard" is a French word for duck. But over the years it has been used to perpetuate a hoax by environmentalists engaged in threats to shut down access to vast deposits of oil that would make the U.S. independent of foreign oil and more specifically, Arabian oil.

The other option is to develop other international oil partnerships. Take Canada for instance. Although the IEA (International Energy Agency), insists that Canada's reserves are limited to 178 billion barrels, many experts - including CEO of Shell Canada, Clive Mather - estimate it to actually be 2 trillion barrels or more. This volume is 8 times more than Saudi Arabia's capacity.

I would rather make our neighbor a lot richer than a suspect country on the other side of the world. Why? It is because many Canadians come to the U.S. for all types of services that help boost the U.S. economy. They maintain a rich trade relationship with us. And, I don't believe they are plotting against the United States to destroy us like some Arab nations.

Besides, some of my best friends are Canadians, and more importantly than that, we are NOT at war with them!

The same argument applies to Mexico. We already import around 47% of their oil exports or 11.4% of our total needs in the United States, according to the Consumer Energy Report issued in 2012, "Where The US Gets Its Oil From?" But international oil dependence is not really where our future lies.

How about oil shale? The United States has the largest known deposits of oil shale in the world, according to the Bureau of Land Management (BLM). This shale holds an estimated 2.175 trillion barrels of potentially recoverable oil. Oil shale does not actually contain oil, but a waxy precursor known as kerosene.

There is no significant commercial production of oil from oil shale in the United States. Why? It is because environmental groups and agencies such as the EPA (Environmental Protection Agency) put roadblocks up at every step in the oil shale development process?

But that's not really where we should go. We should continue to develop technologies to harness solar, natural gas, water and wind power, extract clean coal, develop energy from soy beans and corn, and of course, continue exploring the nuclear highway.

There is so much more potential in these alternative power sources that it seems someone may actually be trying to put the brakes on these technologies in favor of not acquiring new methods and continuing to suck oil until it is depleted. That is absolutely wrong.

How much would you bet that when the day comes that there's no more oil, these same companies will already have cornered the "alternative" fuel markets?

SO HERE IS WHAT I WOULD DO:
- Force the car, truck and vehicle manufacturers, whether here in the United States or in other countries, to design every vehicle sold in the United States and in its territories to average at least 50 miles to the gallon by the year 2020.
- Give special credits until 2020 to those companies who are developing and manufacturing alternative energy methods. (Note: This may not be necessary to issue credits since we would have already abolished Taxes!)
- Pass a law that by 2050, all "new" vehicles must use alternative fuels other than oil.
- Reserve oil production for other uses not related to fuel consumption.
- Highly restrict the Environmental Protection Agency from taking part in granting permits for alternative fuel research.
- Allow each state and county to undertake the permit granting process.
- Allow drilling for oil under strict guidelines, using the latest methods of secure drilling.
- Reserve deep sea drilling as the last alternative for mining oil due to the superiority of other methods.

There is no doubt that good old American-knowhow will rise to the occasion and produce the methods necessary to meet these goals. We have done it many times in the past as we converted form kerosene lamps to the electric bulb, horse-drawn carriages to the automobile, and rolling dial telephones to one-touch screen texting. There's no reason that we can't do it again!

But here is the best incentive. Whatever we decide to do about energy and consumption, we should do it within our borders. Let's make "our own people" wealthy first by keeping our dollars here and not allowing some crazies on the other side of the world to dictate our economy and the way we live.

I wouldn't trust one of them, not King Feisal, not any of those despots in the Middle East to clean my old beat up car, let alone manage the world's economy.

Am I being discriminatory about them? Absolutely not.

I'm being practical because first of all, getting rid of foreign oil will help our citizens enjoy the fruit of new sources of revenue and much lower costs. And second, it will support those who believe and understand our way of life. Nationalist? You betchaa!

CHAPTER 12

Education, Teachers & Reforms
"Sorry, but you're outa here!"

DISCLAIMER - Thank God that there are many more good and excellent teachers than there are the bad ones. But the problem is that it takes just one bad teacher to ruin many lives, which eventually costs individuals, families, states and the federal government dearly.

PROBLEM #1 – There are ineffective and unqualified instructors teaching some of our kids at this very moment.

PROBLEM #2 - In most cases, you cannot terminate a teacher from the classroom because of unions and tenure.

PROBLEM #3 - Even good pay and great benefits won't get you good teachers because the system does not allow it.

Example: Here in California the education department will support a bad teacher over a great teacher because of "tenure" and ignore performance.

PROBLEM #4 – I've heard certain educators in television interviews and on newspaper reports that say that we cannot pack a child's mind with too much study or information because that child will grow up with a lot of hang ups, insecurities, and an overstressed mind. I say: "Bull-Dung times two!"

PROBLEM #5 - Education administrators want to bring everyone to a level scale or a continually lowering common denominator, so no one feels left out. In other words, they work to lower expectations of excellence so a child does not rise above others. In the process, they create a psychological barrier between children. What a bunch of dingle-berry juice!

SOLUTION #1 - Every teacher MUST pass a yearly accreditation test. In other words, they must get relicensed on an annual basis.

Unfortunately, there is no continuity in testing. Some teachers take a BEST (Basic Educational Skills Test) test every three or four years. Regrettably, others work their way around to taking it. Most don't even bother.

SOLUTION #2 – I say that the BEST test must be mandatory for every teacher. Then, based on their yearly score they earn points that will be commensurate with their pay scale. But that's not where it should stop. There is a higher level of grading a teacher.

SOLUTION #3 – How smart are your students? Outstanding teachers, who have excellent records based on their students' scores, will earn more and will be compensated in a higher pay scale, no matter how long they have been teaching. That's really what it all comes down to.

There are excellent teachers with excellent communication skills who do not encourage, excite, or inspire students to be better. They have the mechanics but fail miserably in motivating students.

Conversely, there are educators who in their own quiet, unassuming ways show students the path to higher learning, sometimes without the student really knowing that they are doing so.

I had a priest who was very unassuming, rather quiet and not boisterous. He taught without flare. But he looked into your eyes and dared you to know more than he did. He challenged your inner-self to prove to him that you were smarter than you appeared. How he did it; I don't know. But to this day Father Lopez, my History and Religion teacher, still affects me to be better.

SOLUTION #4 - Teachers who barely pass and/or fail the accreditation tests will be given one year to bring up their grade or be out of a job. These teachers must be required to take quarterly tests to make sure they are progressing. If they fail in any one of those quarters within a year, they should lose their teaching certificates.

SOLUTION #5 – Teach a child as much as you can at an early age including Mathematics, Geography, World History, Political Science and even Advanced Calculus. They can handle it.

I believe that a child's mind is like a big sponge. It will absorb ten times what an adult mind can. It's been proven to me over and over again.

I have a nephew who at the age of three learned to fluently speak English, Spanish and French. To this day (he's now 37) he can still remember all three languages.

SOLUTION #6 - Life is not fair, so let's stop trying to make it so for everyone. Not all of us are born with great looks, terrific bodies and sharp minds. Not all of us have the fortune to have great parents, affluent families and environments tailored to give us the best shot at succeeding. Not everyone has the same mental capacity to learn, decipher and adjust. So we cannot lower expectations so that everyone feels equal.

What we can do, is make the best possible education available to each and every child. Whether a child is able to excel or not has to be left to God. If we invest in providing each child the resources to reach their maximum potential, that's all we can do.

ALLOW ME TO EXPOUND: Anyone who wants to teach must be educated! Dah! Did I say that?

As ridiculous as this statement seems, it's surprising how many teachers are currently teaching in our public school system that are less educated than the students they instruct.

I had an experience with one teacher who sent home a note about my son's behavior in class. I counted no less than twelve spelling and "typo" errors in that short note. I took that note, corrected in red, handed it back to the teacher and discussed my son's behavior as well as the teacher's knowledge of the subject being taught.

I eventually pulled my son from that class. Months later, that teacher was not at that school any longer.

The lack of good teachers is a problem. This is especially true in school districts where teachers are hard to come by or difficult to convince to teach because of the challenges they will face in that district.

I'm talking about those schools where teachers practically have to pack a gun just to get through first period or carry a pencil video camera on their back to keep an eye on the class. In these situations we settle for the alternative: people with guts to stand in front of a white or black board, keep a class under control and attempt to teach while dodging bullets and erasers, even if they (the teachers) don't have the proficiency and skills to educate well.

In fact, these people are more of a "class monitor" than a teacher. I may be exaggerating in my examples, but I'm not far from the truth.

Lest you think these are the only teachers who may be suspect, there are also quite a few teaching in affluent communities who cannot tell you who the current vice president is, or complete a sentence with proper grammatical structure, or divide formulas using more than two digits. This is sad, but true, and I have personally met with several who fit this description.

Teachers are our most valuable resources. The future of our country relies on our educational system and it is most in danger of being bankrupt.

The United States chalks up the lowest scores, worldwide, in several key categories. The U.S. ranks as follows:

Mathematics: Top is Hong Kong, China, and Taiwan; the lowest is Brazil. The U.S. ranks 28th out of thirty countries.

Reading: Top of the pack is Finland and Korea; bottom of the heap is Tunisia, and the U.S. is ranked: 14th of the thirty!

Science: Finland and Hong Kong once again take the top spots with the lowest ranking going to Tunisia once more. The U.S.A. holds the 20th place only eight places above the poorest of the thirty!

Countries such as Finland, China, Japan, The Netherlands, and South Korea usually post in the top ten. These are nations that at one time or another the United States liberated, helped, poured billions and billions of dollars to make their lives better!

You can search the internet to get the latest results (as I did) from a number of sources; however, and unfortunately, the U.S. never lands in the top 10 anymore.

How did that happen? How can a country whose citizens were once so educated, whose understanding was so far-reaching in the sciences, and whose professionals were so amazing at developing new technologies, ever get to the point where we are now? We can't blame it on Communism, we can't blame it on low-paying teacher's jobs, and we can't blame it on an antiquated school system.

So who can we blame? UNIONS! (I have a separate chapter on this topic, but for the time being, allow me to explore a few ideas.)

UNIONS allow weak and unqualified teachers to remain at their job. I don't need to convince you of that because you see the stories on your local station or in your hometown newspaper about teachers who are under investigation. Alleged child abusers and proven incompetent educators remain on the job or paid leave while the education department "investigates" the charges. In the end it seems that these charges are just washed away.

I believe that certain unqualified teachers are like Herpes: You can't get rid of them once you have them. You can treat them temporarily, but incompetent teachers always show up somewhere else infecting other children.

Unfortunately, the good apples have not been separated from the bad. We are not only paying for incompetent teachers, but in the process we are going broke because it's not just their salaries that we have to worry about, but their terrific benefits, including comprehensive medical coverage and their unparalleled retirement pay.

This scale is all skewed.

But I'm going to shock you. The best teachers should get higher pay and a more generous benefits package than almost any other profession. They should certainly be on par with doctors and top executives of large corporations and even our own "hack" politicians. Among all civilian jobs they should be among the top-earners in the United States.

How'd you like that?

On the other hand, the weakest teachers should be shown the door as quickly and expeditiously as possible so that potentially more qualified teachers can join our education system.

I spent my early formative years in public school in Argentina before coming to the United States. When I got here, I was supposed to start in the sixth grade, but because of my low English proficiency was dropped to the 5th grade. That was understandable as the only two words I knew were: yes and no!

That was May 1954. In November of the same year, I was speaking English (albeit with a heavy accent) sufficiently to understand the teacher (a priest) and in return, to be understood by everyone. By February 1955, I was moved up to 6th grade and finished that summer among the top five in my class

They wanted to move me to the 8th grade for the coming September because I was so much more advanced in science, world history, trigonometry, calculus and reading; however, my parents did not allow it. My folks believed that learning English proficiently was more important than showing off in class. Besides, subject matters such as calculus, trigonometry and world geography would not be taught until I moved into the 9th grade.

The moral of my story is that we are wasting those years where a child's mind is primed for learning, when we fail to challenge our children because we want them to be the same as all of the other kids.

As I said before, kids are a dry sponge waiting to be filled. It doesn't hurt them to learn several languages, advanced mathematics, science, world history and how to read and write correctly.

I believe that between the first grade and sixth grade, we've got golden minds to work with. After that, who knows?

I guess this all depends on the parents and how much they allow their children to learn. Tell me how is it that certain parents and teachers can teach children how to swim even before they are walking? I've seen two and three-year-olds reading at seventh or eighth grade levels.

It all starts at home with an environment which embraces education, the finer things of life, art, mathematics, history and current world events. Informative discussions at the dinner table are perhaps the most important ritual that a child can partake in and absorb from an early age.

Yet, how many parents actually sit at the dinner table with their children and converse with each other?

Let me say it again, we have a big problem. There are not enough qualified teachers. Those who are better than average need to be paid more and nurtured to stay in the education system and not bolt for a much better paying job in the corporate world. Facts are facts! And there's the rub.

To further illustrate how important a good teacher is in the life of a person, I have another personal anecdote:

Father Cavalle, the most hated, feared and no-nonsense Jesuit priest ever to teach at our school (St. John Vianney, Los Angeles, CA – an all-boys school), was an S.O.B according to many of us. He was a straightforward guy who was our principal and teacher. You dared not mess around with him. He was a former amateur boxer.

Father Cavalle could literally stop you in the hallways if you were not in the classroom or were caught screwing around during school hours. He would lift you up with one hand under your neck and with the other hand sport a massive, clinched fist and dangle it right in front of your face, just daring you to talk back.

Needless to say, he got the best results from all of us because we could not challenge him. I was one of those students whom he loved to torture (and deservedly so because I was really a screw-up, a jock, and a comedic instigator in all my classes—you know, the class clown). Yet years later, I recognized how important he was in my development.

Father Cavalle was aware of my attitude toward him. So one day after we had a disagreement about my behavior (I insinuated that he was a bully and because he was a priest I could not do anything about it), he said to me; *"Go put on some gloves and meet me in the gym in fifteen minutes."*

I believed that I had every opportunity to get revenge being six-foot, a pretty good athlete and in the prime of my life. I was ready to take him on. One-on-one. Mano-à-Mano.

There was no one to see the "Battle of the Century," but that was OK. I was going to get all my pent-up frustrations and dislike for him out and let him have it.

Of course that didn't happen. He proceeded to beat the crap out of me and had me down on the mat a couple of times. He helped me get up each time and even allowed me to throw the first punch.

He then said to me, "You know, for a Peruvian, you throw a pretty good punch, almost as good as us Italians. But you still have a ways to go. Yet, I see the determination in your face. Use that for the good that it can bring you."

In subsequent days, months and years, we became pretty good friends, and he helped me in my studies. We even sparred at least once a week, just for training purposes.

Some of my buddies were asking how come I was getting along with him and doing well in his class?

I told them that I was taking his classes seriously and if I didn't he would beat the crap out of me.

Truly, what did it for me is that finally, besides my family, there was someone else who cared for me and wanted to see me succeed in life. He was a great teacher.

This was a great lesson in life for me, and even at age seventy, I still remember it as if it was last month.

CHAPTER 13

We lost the Frikin' War!

Today's war on drugs has been lost. Why not surrender? After all, look what prohibition did for the United States in the twenties and thirties. The war on "spirits" (any type of alcohol) in the United States, which lasted between 1920 and 1933 (also known as "The Nobel Experiment") was a total fiasco. Those tumultuous thirteen years cost this country billions, and I'm talking about the 1930's dollars. In today's dollars such a tab could very well mount up trillions.

Not only did Prohibition cost us plenty, but it became a festering wound of new and deadly consequences.

This experiment encouraged more crime than ever before. It made honest working people criminals because they took advantage of a stupid law. It created a vast underground to launder millions and millions of dollars that never saw the light of a tax roll. And it fostered a group of top-tiered criminals. Even today, society still feels their effects.

What a stupid war this was. Example:

The annual budget of the Bureau of Prohibition went from $4.4 million to $13.4 million during the 1920's, while Coast Guard spending on Prohibition averaged over $13 million per year.

As a result, the price of beer increased by more than 700 percent, and that of brandies increased by 433 percent. However, spirit prices increased by only 270 percent, which led to an absolute surge in the consumption of spirits over pre-Prohibition levels.

According to Thomas M. Coffey, who wrote The Long Thirst-Prohibition in America, 1920-1933, there was a tremendous backlash, once the government enforced prohibition. "The death rate from poisoned liquor was appallingly high throughout the country. In 1925 the national toll was 4,154 as compared to 1,064 in 1920. The homicide rate increased to 10 per 100,000 people during the 1920s, a 78 percent increase over the pre-Prohibition period.

Prohibition quickly filled the prisons to capacity. By 1932 the number of federal convicts had increased 561 percent, to 26,589, and the federal prison population had increased 366 percent.

Prohibition not only created the Bureau of Prohibition, it gave rise to a dramatic increase in the size and power of other government agencies as well. Between 1920 and 1930

employment at the Customs Service increased 45 percent, and the service's annual budget increased 123 percent.
Source: The CATO Institute

So, did we learn anything from that period?

It appears that we did not, because we are doing the same thing again, except it's no longer with beer or alcohol. The government earns a handsome amount of tax on these legal drugs.

The Prohibition of the twenty-first century includes cocaine, heroin, marijuana, crack, and a sundry of other drugs that have been making people rich for years...and its *"We the People"* who pay for it!

Does that make any sense to you?

It certainly abhors me to realize that all of those so-called "smart" people in Washington and at the state levels really don't know shit!

THERE IS A LESSON TO BE LEARNED! Make everything legal! Start with marijuana, and work your way through the exotic drugs like cocaine, crystal meth, and heroin on down the line. Because if we think that we can eradicate their use, we are just whistling in the dark.

Addicts and others who want to try these drugs will find ways to get them. This has been proven time after time. In fact, access seems to only have gotten easier.

Oops, I just felt a couple of people throw this book against the wall. Oh, well, I can't satisfy everyone...

PROBLEM: We have all but lost the "War on Drugs" and the costs have been staggering; just as they were back in the twenties and thirties!

How much do you think has been spent to fight the drug war since the Reagan Administration of 1986? Hold on to you seats or something solid nearby. The following estimates are based on averages per year from 1986 to 2011.

In 2003 the government estimated that we had spent $19,000,000,000.00 (those are billions by the way) fighting drugs and the cartels while managing a huge publicity campaign to make sure that everyone knew Nancy Reagan's motto: *"Say NO to Drugs."*

Right now, as I'm writing this portion of the book, the "Drug War Clock" on my computer screen is ticking away. Oops it just changed from $29,032,999,457 to $29,033,031,682 (billion). We still have three months to complete the 2011 year; I'm estimating that figure could be around the $35 billion mark by December 2011.

(Update: We're already into the seventh month of 2012, the clock is registering $28,277,280,775 (billion) for the year and we still have five months to go before the end of 2012.)

These figures represent moneys spent by our Federal and State governments for law enforcement, jails, court costs, etc. We are not counting the collateral expenses of suicides, overdoses, robberies, illnesses as a result of drug use, welfare of families and children left in a lurch by the father or mother, or a number of other related problems.

Not included is the incarceration of 1.2 million drug offenders, of the 2 million-plus inmates we currently house in our prisons. Needless to say, those amounts are unbelievable as well.

If we have spent an average of $20B per year since 1986 to the present that represents (let me take my shoes off), a gigantic $40,000,000,000,000.00! If you don't want to count all those zeroes, that's $40 trillion dollars (easier for people like me who cipher on ten toes and ten fingers!!!) I have a headache already and this chapter is barely started.

Imagine what we could do with that kind of money or better yet, what we could have done with that money for the past 25 years. We would not be in the same *boat-at-sea-without-a-paddle* situation as we are today.

The sad thing is that we still have as many drug addicts and drug related crimes as before. Our attempts to squelch drug distribution and use have been somewhat useless. Moreover, in the process of conducting this unwinnable war, we have made billionaires of thousands of people (politicians included) whose names you're going to need lessons in French, Zulu and of course Spanish, to pronounce.

The top ten billionaire drug lords include: (a few may have been killed or incarcerated, but their cartel remains alive and still pushing the limits)

No. 10 - "Freeway" Ricky Ross, operating in the Western United States. Cocaine is his game. He's running the cartel from his prison cell.

No. 9 - Paul Lira Alexander, a.k.a. "The Baron of Cocaine" from Brazil, he services mostly U.S. clients. New York, Los Angeles and Chicago are his main customers.

No. 8 - Santiago Luis Polanco Rodriguez, a.k.a. "Yayo" operating from the U.S. with clients here, in Jamaica and the Dominican Republic. Crack cocaine is his calling.

No. 7 - Felix Mitchell, a.k.a. "The Cat" a good old boy from the U.S. heavily invested in heroin and crack cocaine.

No. 6 - Who can forget **Carlos Lehder,** who operates from the Bahamas, but sells cocaine mainly to the U.S.?

No. 5 - Jose Gonzalo Rodriguez Gacha, the toast of the town in Columbia, who deals in most Latin/French regions: North, Central and South America, the Caribbean, Western Europe and Asia. Care for a coke?

No. 4 - And then we have the beautiful **Griselda Blanco, a.k.a. The "Cocaine Queen of Miami"** who is as ruthless as Al Capone, Joe Bonnano, John Gotti and Carlo Gambino, all put together. She killed among many, a 2 year-old child. This finally led the DEA to catch her. She was convicted for 20 years but released in 2004 and immediately deported to Columbia. No one knows her whereabouts but I can bet you that she is living "large."

No. 3 - Khun Sa, a.k.a. "The Opium King" makes his headquarters out of Burma, but primarily sells to the U.S. and specifically New York where he supplied over 80% of the heroine sold. Opium is his taste of choice. In the late 90s, he opted to turn himself over to Burmese officials and not risk being extradited to the U.S. When the New York judge ordered a warrant for his arrest and extradition, he just laughed. He died at the age of 73 of natural causes in Yangon, Myanmar, Burma.

No. 2 - Armando Carrillo Fuentes, a.k.a. The "Lord of the Skies," lives in Mexico and trades in pure cocaine in Mexico, the United States, Argentina and Chile. He is credited for being the first of such criminals to have a fleet of 727 airplanes to make deliveries.

And the number one kingpin is...

No. 1 - The late **Pablo Escobar,** Columbia's own Godfather, who tied up North, Central and South America drug traffic for himself. He had been supplying over 80% of heroin to the U.S. and other countries as well as the Columbian government for years.

After much pressure from the United States and around the world, the Columbian government decided to do something about Pablo. The crafty "Narco-Man" negotiated a sweetheart deal with Columbia's government to build him a prison that would be considered a five-star hotel anywhere in the world. He went to "jail" on his own accord to appease the world and lived a happy life in luxury.

Under his stronghold it is estimated that over 3,000 people died in Columbia and in other parts of the world.

Although eventually caught and shot by DEA agents, he's not forgotten, and his tentacles still extend throughout Columbia, the United States and many other Latin-American countries.

SOLUTION: We could get rid of the United States, which is the main bread basket for all these impresarios. No more United States, no more market -- these clowns and their families would have to go back to pushing carts and selling *"Chiclets"* at the border crossings. Facetious? Of course.

SOLUTION #2: Make every drug, I mean every drug (and include prostitution and gambling in that new law), **legal!** Done deal! Problem solved.

The good old U.S. Government, and especially today's zealous administration, can finally realize its wishes. It can take on an enterprise, control it, massage it and make a lot of money out of it. Leave everything else to private enterprise.

This can happen within 48 hours. President Obama, you can finally get your wish and run a business where we don't need to get involved.

THE OUTSTANDING BENEFITS OF MAKING EVERY KIND OF DRUG, LEGAL:

1. To start, you will drive all cartels out of business. The cartel would have to sell their product for less than it costs to manufacture because the American entrepreneurial spirit would lead to companies producing legitimate "illegal" drugs while paying taxes and selling them through numerous legitimate outlets. No need for any shady characters "dealing" in the back parking lots.

2. Drug companies, who would most likely buy from producers who have been cleared by the government, will make more money. Following the outline of the "Painless Progressive Tax" they and others will have already paid taxes at every sector of drug manufacturing, distributing and retail. Drug prices, due to market competition, will be kept low enough

to make it practically impossible for any individual to try to manufacture or import the stuff as cheaply as the legitimate companies can produce it.

3. Legalizing all drugs creates a huge tax base. Imagine collecting taxes on 60 to 80 billion dollars a year of product? Perhaps even more because the manufacturer, the retailer and then the consumer all pay taxes--a triple play, I'd say.

4. Many American farmers would have the opportunity to plant high-yield, lucrative crops. Envision bumper crops of coco leaves, poppies and other plants needed for drug production.

5. All the taxes derived from growing, manufacturing and selling drugs would include a portion allocated to a "National Healthcare Program." No, this is not a healthcare program only for addicts. Instead, the funds from these drug sales could provide coverage to every single man, woman and child who lives under the poverty level and who does not have their own insurance program. That money, along with the contributions made by each insurance company in America to feed that fund, would more than suffice to keep up with the costs of medical care. We are talking billions folks. Billions!

6. The "druggies" finally would be contributing to society while also indulging themselves.

7. Some say that at first, funeral homes and crematoriums would be full of people who overdosed. I don't agree because this did not happen when the alcohol laws were repealed after Prohibition. So it does not necessarily follow that

drug addicts will use more when it is legal. Perhaps the death pool may increase for the first few years but then it will level off, just as it has with the use of alcohol. And again, the government is not responsible for individuals. The individual and his/her family and circle of friends are the first-line of prevention and support for an addict, not the state.

8. Taxing drugs of all kinds will raise money to spend on social issues, education, sports, the arts, etc. Remember, 40 trillion over 25 years can go a long way.

9. You will also have enough money to put people like lawbreakers Armando Carrillo Fuentes, Sra. Griselda Blanco, Khun Sa, and others, in a home for old cartel honchos. You can call this place the "Hotel Cartel for Senior Druggies." However, I dare say that these same people, once drugs are legitimatized, may turn out to be honest law abiding citizens.

   I can think of one example: Joe Kennedy. He was one of the biggest bootleggers during Prohibition, and the patriarch of the Kennedy Family, who most citizens of the United States consider America's Royal Family. He became legitimate. So much so that he was named Ambassador to England and the Royal Court. Now, there's a switch.

BUT WHAT ABOUT PROSTITUTION & GAMBLING?

Although these could have their own dedicated chapters, I believe these two topics fit here.

They say that "Prostitution" is the oldest profession in the world. I believe it.

I cannot pin-point with any kind of certainty when it exactly became illegal, but the fact that it has progressed and continued for all these centuries, only tells me that there's got to be something more to sex-for-sale than anyone is willing to admit. Laws have not affected this market much. The attraction to sex is so strong that prostitution just will never go away. So why not tax it?

Legal prostitution will mean "cleaner sex" according to Dr. OZ of the TV show by the same name. It will also be "safe sex" as both participants would need to provide some type of current medical affidavit or exam before making the purchase or selling it.
 Collecting taxes from "Johns" and "Janes" would mean millions of dollars in the country's coffer, which in turn would trickle-down to state and local governments.

GAMBLING – That problem is almost gone since every city, county and state allows gambling of one sort or another, in addition to Las Vegas and Atlantic City. The new computerized gambling and gaming options are spreading like wild flowers, so let the government make all these legal and collect the taxes! That simple.

Another problem solved.
Next...

CHAPTER 14

Unions
(Why?)

It has been said, "Be careful what you wish for, you just might get it." Or the all-time gem, "That's too good to be true!"

 When it comes to unions of any kind, the above phrases seem to fit like a glove.

PROBLEM: Unions have caused businesses to leave the United States in favor of more productive and less expensive overhead costs. Many businesses go to third-world countries (Although I wouldn't call China a third-world country even though 90% of its people live as if they were in a third-world society).

Unions also cost huge amounts of money to maintain. But it doesn't end there.

Once a person has retired from his/her work, they become wards of the unions. While working, these people basically give up their inherent rights for the sake of union protection. They cannot go against a union edict or they risk being dropped like a lead weight; which impacts the member's life before and after retirement.

The concept of unionizing, the original concept, mind you, was lost long ago. Today unions have morphed into something so abstract, amorphous and in some cases, deadly, that there are few limits available to contain them.

Unions are like a Venus Fly Trap which needs to be fed continuously. The larger it gets the hungrier and more demanding it gets.

SOLUTION: Limit union responsibilities to certain basic matters including working conditions, safety measures, and reasonable hours; then let the marketplace take care of the rest.

Crazy? I don't think so. You are talking to a guy that at one time belonged to three different unions. I still keep one of my union cards current.

A few years back I belonged to the Musicians Union, AFTRA (American Federation of Television and Recording Artists), and SAG (Screen Actors Guild) (AFTRA & SAG have since merged). These cards were all a must for me to have if I wanted to continue working in those careers. So I paid my dues and supported their efforts and kept working.

However, even back in the mid-seventies, when I first joined the unions, I thought that there was something wrong with the concept.

I remember working as an actor at MGM and seeing a set of lights attached to an electrical cord fall and become stuck on a receptacle and eventually unplug. I moved to help and get everything back in order. Suddenly I was terribly chastised by a lighting man for trying to help and do someone else's job.

I was told, *"You are fucking taking the job of another person. Don't do that, asshole."* At first I felt ashamed for taking someone else's job away. That was never my intention. But I thought it was ludicrous for me to sit back and let someone else do the work that I could have easily done, or at least helped complete.

Unions became important when workers were being taken advantage of by greedy company owners and managers who directed lower level administrators to suck every single drop of blood, sweat and tears out of a person for as little pay as possible.

Overtime was unheard of. The mentality was, "We have a job for you, take it or we'll get someone else."

And when an executive heard this coming from a laborer, the outcome was usually unpleasant: *"You want what? You want a ten minute break so that you can get a cup of water or coffee or go to the bathroom? Are you crazy? I'm not paying you to relieve yourself. Do it on your own time."*

Or, *"Get the hell out of my office, you ungrateful clown. A raise? Who do you think you are? Henry Ford?"*

There was a legitimate need for people to unionize themselves in order to fight for nothing more than better working conditions and respect from their bosses.

Employees who get ill because of working conditions or incur injuries because of the job they do, have proper and legitimate claims. Each worker has the right to be protected.

Once upon on time, the need for unions was real. During those years, I'll go as far as saying that unions were an integral part of our work force and eventually helped make this country's labor force great.

But what happened between the time when those needs were met and today?

"Union Armageddon" I call it. It's like the old saying, "You give someone an inch and they'll take a mile."

Unions are a direct cause of poor workmanship and laziness in the work place (including teachers, police, fire fighters, assembly line workers, electricians, plumbers, etc.). They make ridiculous demands, have participated in or encouraged criminal acts, and are contributing to the current destruction of our economic system.

Many union locals force companies, cities, states and governments to pass on the higher costs of doing business to the consumer. As a result, companies move elsewhere; mostly out of the country, to produce their goods at a more reasonable cost.

In the case of social and human services, we are forced to meet their demands while trying to pay for them one way or another. Here in California, we suffer the consequences. Unions are ruining the state.

Wait! They have actually ruined this state.

Ultimately, what good does it do for the workforce, the consumer, and the country, for a union to demand outrageous pay scales, golden benefits and almost absurd retirement plans?

It's the union bosses and their attorneys who really benefit from this arrangement; everyone else is left behind, cannot opt out, or are pressed to deal with modernization and made to feel useless.

Just looking at CEO salaries for the years 2009-2010 for some of the top unions, will give you an idea why they are always asking for more money:

- The **National Education Association** – 3.2 million members. Its president, Dennis Van Roekel, was paid a salary of $397,721.
- **Service Employees International Union** – 1.8 million members working in hospital, nursing homes, local and state and federal government jobs, etc. Its president, Andy Stern was paid $306,388 plus benefits.
- **United Food & Commercial Workers** – 1.3 million members. President Joseph T. Hansen received an annual salary of $360,737. More than that when adding benefits and bonuses.

- **The American Federation of Teachers** – 887K strong. Randi Weingarten, who was elected president in 2008, earned a whopping $428,284 per year.

The business of running a union is quite good.

I'm not clueless as to what I'm suggesting.

Remember, I still carry a union card. My son-in-law is a member of three unions in the film and television industries and has hundreds of friends who have benefitted from their respective unions. I know first-hand how important it has been for him and his career.

Even so, I believe the time has come to get back to the ground level of reality and re-think this whole matter, or we will continue losing jobs to some other place on this planet and our economic woes and social shortfalls will be ten-times larger than they are.

As a writer and promoter, I take risks and produce. I have no union affiliate to back me up, so I must be cognizant that I must save for my eventual retirement, health care and doctor's visits and still pay my bills (so I'll never retire). I do have Medicare and supplemental insurance which I pay for every month.

Would I like to have everything covered so that I don't have to pay that extra medical supplemental coverage? Of course, but the realities are that if I want my wife and I to be properly covered in our later years, I need to continue to work and be productive.

So what's wrong with that? In years past, I would have been lucky if I lived past 62 years-old. Today the average life expectancy for me is around 80. For women, that average is

86 years-old. What this means to me is that I have no time to feel sorry for myself or wait on someone else to take care of my needs. I must do it myself.

My lovely wife of fifty-plus years, at 68 years-old, works three days a week not just to help with our finances, but also to keep healthy. She can't get sick. She's got far too many responsibilities. And the bottom line is that we both feel good about being able to continue to contribute to society.

Unions however, continue to negotiate as if our life span was still 62 years-old. So the fact that older citizens collect pensions, social security, and unemployment up to an average of 76 years of age and beyond, skews the current formula. It needs to be changed. But we'll deal with that in the Social Security segment of this book.

In the meantime, I believe that all union contracts must be renegotiated now, not three or four years from now. Our economy is so much in the tank that if we don't do anything about it immediately, we will be facing the same problems Spain, Greece and heaven forbid, France are facing.

France is clueless. As the country faces economic disaster, their new Socialist President just enacted a law to "lower" the retirement age. Yes, I said "lower it." This means that there are now several more millions of people ready to extend their collective hands out to the government while asking, "Give me more, give me more."

How ridiculous is that?

Wait, I'm speaking of France, I should know better. Sorry.

CHAPTER 15

Social Security & Retirement Age

PROBLEM: Social Security is running out of money.

SOLUTION: Change the age for retirement.

Solved! How is that for the KISS principle?

During the current debates between Republican presidential hopefuls, one candidate made big news by proclaiming the Social Security concept as a "Ponzi Scheme."

The liberal media jumped all over that statement and the candidate who said it. The "main-stream-media" is so hungry for bad news from the Republican sector that in their rush to cover the headlines and print banners across the TV screen, they overlooked what that statement meant.

Definition of Ponzi (Wikipedia):

> *A **Ponzi scheme** is a fraudulent investment operation that pays returns to its investors from their own money or the money paid by subsequent investors, rather than from any actual profit earned by the individual or organization running the operation.*

Can you tell me where this statement is inconsistent with what we do with Social Security?

1. American workers start paying into the Social Security fund early in their working life, with the promise that when we retire, we will get a portion of what we have paid-in, back.

2. Since the moneys paid into our Social Security fund are not invested but are used to take care of those who started paying their Social Security earlier; it's always working on a "negative" balance. The fund always needs more currency, cash, and mullah to keep up with the demand.

3. As a result, we are using moneys paid by Paul to pay Peter (who has been there longer).

4. Unless more people keep paying into the fund, it will run out of money soon because of another factor...

5. When "Social Security" was first introduced in August 14, 1935 and first enacted in 1940, people's average life expectancy was 65. There was not a strain on the system because the government did not need to pay as many people for so many years. But we are living well into our seventies now by taking

advantage of new medicines and healthier customs that allow people to live well beyond the life expectancies of the 1930's. Therefore, Social Security needs to change with the times.

So what is the difference between Charles (Carlo) Ponzi's Scheme and Social Security? None!

SOLUTIONS:

I believe that as we pay our Social Security, shares of that money should be invested on our behalf into government owned financial instruments to earn the highest possible return. Even though these returns may not be as great as profits earned in the open market; investments in the government carry little risks to the investor. Unless, of course, our country goes down the tubes and then we're all in on the same sinking ship.

In order to take care of the huge deficits in Social Security; the best solution is to make immediate change.

1. Change the retirement age from 62 to 65 years-old for people who are presently 50 years-old or younger.
2. Change the Medicare program of benefits from 62 to 65 years-old.
3. For every year that a person does not collect Social Security after 65 years-old, increase individual benefits by a certain percentage. (I'll let heady economists and their sharp minds figure out the appropriate percentage.)

4. Anyone with a net income of $500,000 per annum should be given the option to refuse Social Security benefits and qualify to have a street named after them. Silly, but it might just work.

Implementing these changes will have an instant impact on our economy. It will NOT hurt those who are fifty-one years old and older, who were counting on retiring at 62. They still will qualify and can count on their retirement plans. On the other hand the forty-something's and younger will have at least fifteen years to prepare for the change.

That seems fair to me. Problem solved.
What's next?

CHAPTER 16

Credit Card Companies & Banks
Law breakers! Why?

PROBLEM: People fall behind on their credit payments because of legitimate emergencies, educational costs and other mounting expenses. It's not unheard of that credit card companies come down hard and charge as much as 35% interest on the outstanding debt.

You and I can be jailed for charging anyone more than 10% per annum. We would be charged with "usury." That's a big no, no.

So how come the laws regarding usury do not apply to certain credit card companies, banks and lenders?

Credit card companies can basically charge what they want in interest.

According to a published article by Lucy Lazarony at www.bankrate.com:

Less than half of all U.S. states bother to cap credit card interest rates, and few credit card issuers are based in these states anyway.

Most major credit card issuers are based in states without usury laws and without interest rate caps on credit cards. Banks and credit card issuers based in these states can charge any interest rate they wish -- as long as the rate is listed in the cardholder agreement and the borrower agrees.

And thanks to a 1978 U.S. Supreme Court decision, these the-sky's-the-limit rate policies dominate the credit card business."

SOLUTION? Put a cap on interest rates in every State. Or, tear up all your credit cards.

Well, we all know that's not always possible.

PRACTICALITY: I keep one or two credit cards just in case of emergencies. This seems wise when we face times when I may have to borrow money to get through the week, fix the broken water line under the house, come up with the ever increasing school tuition, the unexpected doctor's visit, or to pick up the medicine my family needs.

At times like these you say, "Fuck-it" to the world. "I've got to do what I have to do and I'll worry about paying it later."

Unfortunately, at that moment, the banks and credit card companies have got you. One purchase leads to another even though you'll say to yourself, "It's only another hundred dollars or basically another $10 added to my monthly payment. No big deal."

Before you know it you find yourself with a noose around your neck. They have you strung up on a branch." Now you are working just to pay the high interest sometimes for life, unless you declare bankruptcy.

It is bad enough that in emergencies you have to resort to buying items on credit because you need them. It is even worse that banks and credit card companies go beyond the laws that apply to everyone else in this country and require exorbitant interest rates.

SOLUTION: The government should only allow credit card companies and banks to charge the legal interest rate that everyone else is required to charge and no more. If the legal limit is 10%, then that's what it should be for everyone. Anything higher than that should be illegal.

Why are they allowed to charge more in interest and penalties that the average citizen cannot? I have yet to receive an honest answer from a banker, lending officer, credit card manager, or someone in India or Taiwan who handles my Visa or Master Card account here in the United States.

I know that these companies move their credit card division to states where there is no "usury" laws and can charge what they want. Neat!

Fortunately, my new vision for elections and term limits and the "grading" of politicians by constituents; should take care of that problem quickly. Politicians won't need to depend on the credit card lobby to acquire reelection funds…since they cannot be reelected. Therefore, politicians can move to pass legislation to curtail the high interest charged and make it an even playing field for everyone.

With overages in our budget and the way we collect taxes along the way, we can probably set up an "Emergency Bank Card" that would provide one-time credit at very low interest rates for people who need it at once.

Simple!

CHAPTER 17

A National Day for Elections

PROBLEM: Many citizens of the United States do not vote when they have the opportunity. Others, who do vote, should not because they don't know enough to cast educated well-informed ballots.

SOLUTION: Make everyone cast a well-informed vote or exact penalties. If a voter cannot answer five or six basic questions regarding politics at the local, state or federal level, their voting rights should be postponed for that election.

It's too easy for people to not vote because they are lazy, don't care, or just don't like any of the candidates. WRONG! BIG TIME WRONG!

If we wish to keep our country alive and vital in the world, we must exercise our right to vote anytime we have the opportunity. Each person must take their vote seriously.

Unfortunately, those who don't exercise their right use the poorest of excuses...one of them being: I could not get off work!

Unless you are enslaved by your job and are caged in your little cubby-hole, you can find sufficient time to go and vote at the nearest polling location.

As easy as the government makes it, many U.S. citizens fail to see the wisdom in exercising their unalienable right to vote.

Therefore, I'm calling for extreme measures. I have argued that everyone who votes must be knowledgeable as to who or what they are voting for. This chapter moves on and covers the voting process, and whether you like it or not, I think we have arrived at a moment in time where this solution must be considered. NO MORE EXCUSES!

I propose that the last weekends in March and October are dedicated to ELECTIONS from Saturday morning at 6 a.m. until Sunday evening at 10 p.m.

During those two days, everything in the newspapers, on the radio or on television will be reserved for candidates running for public office; whether at the local, city, county, state or federal level. Why would the media allow this or be required to offer this unique request by the government? It is part of the broadcasting and publishing licensing process in the United States.

On radio and television broadcasts, at a specified schedule, candidates will be permitted to present their positions and proposals in local, county, state and national feeds. Since there is absolutely nothing programmed other than political issues; it is likely folks will spend time learning more about the politics of the nation. The print media will dedicate so many pages to local, state and federal candidates as well.

No, this is not punishment, but it may be a way to get this country going in the right direction. Voters need to be savvy. In Chapter 1, we covered how our Constitution will have to be amended to reflect the massive changes I'm suggesting. I say the value of our independence, more than justifies what we spend on our political process.

For the first time, the entire country will be given the opportunity to focus on one thing and one thing only, the future of our government at every level.

Freedom is not free; you must invest in it. It's a wonderful thing to be an American.

CHAPTER 18

Right to Life? - Right to Choose?
Only you and your God can decide.

Who is to say what the solution to this problem is? NOT ME!

Statistics don't bode well for children of a single parent (this is the demographic where most abortions occur); especially when that single parent is a young mother of meager means.

Do we really want a child born to an uneducated teenager who has yet to comprehend the realities of life? Do we want to expose a child to the harshness of living in less than acceptable conditions?

Surely there are children who survive these inequities and make something of themselves. They become solid contributors to society.

There are children who survive because the state places them in good foster homes or with stable families through the adoption process.

These are positive stories that ameliorate concerns over children born to unwed, young mothers. But looking at the existing records and statistics, such success stories are few and far apart.

Nonetheless, again, I go by statistics and records and these indicators don't look promising.

But who are we to decide for another person? Who are we to make a person have a child and then take it away? <u>We do not have that right.</u>

Anyone who thinks God or religion has given them such authority is completely wrong and misusing faith to intervene and bully others. That is absolutely incorrect, my friends.

In the end the person with the child and her husband or lover (if he is around), must decide. Perhaps the family, a priest or rabbi or other religious leader can act as a consultant, advisor or facilitator, but only the mother bearing the child has the last word in the matter. That's her right to decide and no one else's.

The unborn child has no voice in the matter. A woman is in charge of her body and only she can make this decision and then learn to live with the consequences.

If you have religion and believe in God and a Final Judgment, then you must accept such an idea because ultimately, only God will judge.

CHAPTER 19

Excise the EPA Tumor
(Environmental Protection Agency…NOT!)

The EPA is an example of another good idea gone terribly, terribly bad. I've saved this topic for one of the last chapters because after you read their agenda, and understand the overwhelming power of the EPA, you will think that none of the ideas I have suggested in this book will ever work as long as they are around.

The EPA has become the single most creativity-stifling, obstructionist agency in this country. This agency has jurisdiction over almost everything ranging from lipstick for women, hair lotion, Twinkies, bread, shaving cream, and buttons; to manufacturing, home-building and municipal construction, recreational land development, and the establishment of industries that could employ hundreds or thousands of people.

The EPA tumor is a destructive outgrowth of the government. It stifles our society and our economic growth, while claiming to protect us through its various demands and regulations. The dreaded EPA and the assorted branches it regulates, including the Bureau of Land Management (BLM), Bureau of Fish and Game, and Bureau of Fish and Wildlife works together with other environmental wacko fringe groups such as Friends of Earth, the Sierra Club, and hundreds of others, to act for our own good. Yeah, sure.

I'll believe it when the day comes that the government steps aside and gives the reins back to the people.

The idea of environmental protection was and is a good one. But at what point does it becomes useless and at what point is it self-serving?

The EPA employs many people who throw around power. These people work to make you and I work harder than we need to by compelling us to fill-in a plethora of forms and sometimes meaningless tasks. Their job depends on just how much they make us work.

Are these folks really concerned about the environment? I don't think so. If you just add up all the unproductive paperwork they create, the total mass would line-up from here to kingdom-come if it were stacked in a single pile.

At what point are growth, ingenuity, and entrepreneurship terribly hampered and stifled?

Progress is stagnant because of the thousands of laws and regulations that bog down production in this nation, while creating pressure on companies, who after all are looking for profits, to send businesses packing to other countries like China, India and so on.

Who suffers? We do folks, because innovators with ideas to develop, jobs to create, and a vision for the future, spend years trying to get past EPA obstacles in order to just get things started.

This is serious folks...you better be aware of what's going on.

I dare say that Lisa P. Jackson, the current administrator of the Environmental Protection Agency, is the most powerful person in the United States; even more powerful than the President.

Can you digest that?

The following list gives you an idea of the power and reach of the EPA. I don't expect you to read up on everything that is listed, but the extent of their programming drives my point across by demonstrating how pervasive this cancer is in our lives.

As you survey the list, please note that I have underlined those areas which include from fifty to over one hundred sub-sub-headings and almost countless pages of detailing information.
  All of this is mind-boggling, to say the least.
  I believe that it would take the average person a year or so, devoting at least six to eight hours a day, to study and understand each topic, subtopic and subsequent detail.

So with great regret, I present you with the core areas of jurisdiction for the EPA (Environmental Protection Agency). Remember, each heading has an abundance of sub-headings and each of those have even more sub-headings, and on and on and on.

For future reference, here is the link that will take you to the EPA's main webpage as of the spring of 2012:

http://www.epa.gov/lawsregs/sectors/ ,

Here they are...

Agriculture:

Air
National Emissions Standards for Hazardous Air Pollutants (NESHAP):
Pesticide Active Ingredient Production Industry
Industrial, Commercial and Institutional Boilers and Process Heaters

General
Agriculture Laws: including EPA's Regulatory Matrix for agricultural producers.
Agriculture Proposed Rules, Policies and Guidance - Open for Comment
Pasture, Rangeland, and Grazing Operations - Laws, Regulations, Policies, and Guidance

Pesticides
Regulating Antimicrobial Pesticides
Regulating Biopesticides
Regulating Pesticides: Laws & Regulations
Worker Protection Standard (WPS)

Water
Effluent Guidelines: Aquatic Animal Production Industry
National Pollutant Discharge Elimination System (NPDES): Animal Feeding Operations (AFOs): information about agricultural activities regulated by wastewater permits.

Compliance
Agriculture Sector Compliance Assistance:
including sector profiles and assistance centers.
Combustion Portal: compliance assistance center.
Concentrated Animal Feeding Operations (CAFOs) Compliance Monitoring

Enforcement
National Enforcement Initiatives: Preventing Animal Waste from Contaminating Surface and Ground Waters

Policies and Guidance
Agriculture Proposed Rules, Policies and Guidance - Open for Comment
Agriculture Policies and Guidance Collection
NPDES: Concentrated Animal Feeding Operations Guidance Documents:
wastewater permitting information.
Pesticide Regulatory Action Fact Sheets

Forestry and Logging

Laws and Regulations

National Emissions Standards for Hazardous Air Pollutants (NESHAP*): Industrial, Commercial and   Institutional Boilers and Process Heaters*

Compliance

Agriculture Compliance Assistance Center: Forestry Combustion Portal: compliance assistance   center. Sector Notebook: Profile of the Lumber and   Wood Products Industry (PDF) (126 pp, 507 K)

Policies and Guidance

Polluted Runoff: Forestry: managing nonpoint   source   pollution   from   forestry activities.

Construction

Laws and Regulations

Air

Asbestos: Laws and Regulations

National Emissions Standards for Hazardous Air Pollutants (NESHAP): Asbestos

Ozone Layer Protection - Regulatory Programs: including information about stationary and motor vehicle air-conditioning and refrigeration regulations (HVAC and MVAC).

General

Federal Environmental Requirements for Construction (PDF) (8 pp)

Lead

Lead in Paint, Dust, and Soil: Laws and Regulations

Waste

Industrial Waste: Construction and Demolitions Materials

Water

Storm water Discharges from Construction Activities

Effluent Limitation Guidelines: Construction and Development

Compliance

Air

Clean Construction USA: promotes reduction of diesel emissions from construction vehicles and equipment

Complying with the 608 Refrigerant Recycling Rule: air conditioning and refrigeration regulations.
Indoor air PLUS Construction Specifications

General

Construction Sector Compliance Assistance
List of Compliance Assistance Tools for Construction Sites (PDF) (41 pp)
Managing Your Environmental Responsibilities: A Planning Guide for Construction and Development (MYER) (PDF) (225 pp, 2386 K)
New Buildings and Infrastructure Compliance Resources

Lead

Lead Hotline: The National Lead Information Center

Waste

Industrial Materials Recycling: Construction and Demolitions Materials: reducing and recycling C&D materials.
RCRA in Focus: Construction, Demolition, and Renovation (PDF) (24 pp, 1.5MB): A guide for small business, includes a hazardous waste table of RCRA requirements and answers to frequently asked questions.

Enforcement

Home Builders Clean Water Settlement
Reducing Widespread Air Pollution from the   Largest Sources, especially the Coal-Fired Utility, Cement, Glass, and Acid Sectors: National Enforcement Initiatives.

Policies and Guidance

Construction Compliance Documents

Healthcare and Social Assistance

Laws and Regulations

Air

Essential Uses of CFCs for Metered-Dose Inhalers: EPA's yearly notice requesting applications from companies who seek allowances to produce or import CFCs for use as propellant in metered-dose inhalers.
National Emission Standards for Hazardous Air Pollutants (NESHAP): air toxics regulations:

Commercial Sterilizers
Hospital / Medical / Infectious Waste Incinerators (HMIWI)
Hospital Ethylene Oxide Sterilizers (area sources)
Industrial, Commercial and Institutional Boilers and Process Heaters
Pharmaceutical Production Industry

Reciprocating Internal Combustion Engines (RICE), including area sources

Pesticides

Selected EPA-registered Disinfectants: The use of EPA registered products effective against human blood borne pathogens listed are in compliance with OSHA's (Occupational Safety and Health Administration) Occupational Exposure to blood borne Pathogens (29 CFR 1910).

Waste

Medical Waste and *State Medical Waste Programs and Regulations*

Water

Dental Amalgam Effluent Guidelines: reducing discharges of mercury in wastewater.

Pharmaceutical Manufacturing Effluent Guidelines

Compliance

Combustion Portalhttp://www.epa.gov/epahome/exitepa.htm: compliance assistance center.

Healthcare Sector Compliance Assistance: including sector profiles and assistance centers.

Tribal Compliance Assistance Center: Healthcare

Aerospace

Laws and Regulations

Air:

National Emission Standards for Hazardous Air Pollutants (NESHAP):

Asbestos

Chromium Electroplating

Degreasing Organic Cleaners (Halogenated Solvent Cleaners)

Engine Test Cells/Stands (Combined with Rocket Testing Facilities)

Friction Products Manufacturing

Metal Can (surface coating)

Metal Coil (surface coating)

Metal Furniture (surface coating)

Misc. Metal Parts and Products (surface coating)

Paper and Other Web (surface coating)

Plastic Parts (surface coating)

Reinforced Plastic Composites Production

Stratospheric Ozone Regulations:

The Phaseout of Ozone Depleting Substances

Significant New Alternatives Policy (SNAP) Program: EPA's program to evaluate and regulate substitutes for the ozone-depleting chemicals that are being phased out under the stratospheric ozone protection provisions of the Clean Air Act (CAA).

Water:

Airport Deicing Effluent Guidelines

Compliance

Aerospace Sector Compliance Assistance: including industry profiles, compliance assistance centers, and more.

Combustion Portal: compliance assistance center.

Enforcement

US EPA Airline Settlement Information

Related Business Sectors

Transportation

Chemical Manufacturing

Laws and Regulations

Air:

National Emission Standards for Hazardous Air Pollutants (NESHAP):

Benzene Waste Operations

Cellulose Products Manufacturing

Commercial Sterilizers

Ferromanganese and Silicomanganese Production (Ferroalloys, Major Sources)

Generic MACT (Acetal Resins, Hydrogen Floride, Polycarbonates Production, Acrylic/Modacrylic Fibers, Spandex Production, Carbon Black, and Ethylene Processes)

Hazardous Waste Combustion

Hazardous Organic NESHAP (Synthetic Organic Chemical Manufacturing Industry)

Hydrochloric Acid Production (Fumed Silica Production)

Industrial Cooling Towers

Magnetic Tape (surface coating)

Mercury Cell Chlor-Alkali Plants

Misc. Coating Manufacturing

Misc. Organic Chemical Production and Processes (MON)

Organic Liquids Distribution (non-gasoline)

Pesticide Active Ingredient Production
Pharmaceuticals Production
Phosphoric Acid/Phosphate Fertilizers
Polyether Polyols Production
Polymers & Resins I (Butyl Rubber, Epichlorohydrin Elastomers, Ethylene Propylene Rubber, Hypalon (TM), Neoprene, Nitrile Butadiene, Polybutadiene Rubber, Polysulfide, and Styrene-Butadiene Rubber and Latex)
Polymers & Resins II (Epoxy Resins and Non-Nylon Polyamides)
Polymers & Resins III (Amino and Phenolic Resins)
Polymers & Resins IV (Acrylonitrile-Butadiene-Styrene, Methyl Methacrylate-Acrylonitrile+, Methyl Methacrylate-Butadiene++, Polystrene, Styrene Acrylonitrile, Polyethylene Terephthalate, and Nitrile Resins)
Polyvinyl Chloride and Copolymers Production
Primary Copper
Reinforced Plastic Composites Production
Site Remediation
Tetrahydrobenzaldehyde Manufacture (Formerly Butadiene Dimers Production)

Stratospheric Ozone Regulations:
The Phaseout of Ozone Depleting Substances
Significant New Alternatives Policy (SNAP) Program - EPA's program to evaluate and regulate substitutes for the ozone-depleting chemicals that are being phased out under the stratospheric ozone protection provisions of the Clean Air Act (CAA).

Toxic Substances:
Chemical Information Collection and Data Development (Testing) - requirements for manufacturers and processors of existing chemicals to test their chemicals for health and environmental effects.
New Chemicals Program- Established to help manage the potential risk from chemicals new to the marketplace. Mandated by Section 5 of TSCA.

Water:
Potential Chlorine and Chlorinated Hydrocarbon (CCH) Manufacturing Guidelines: effluent guidelines.
Organic Chemicals, Plastics, and Synthetic Fibers (OCPSF): effluent guidelines.

Compliance

Chemical Manufacturing Sector Compliance Assistance: including industry profiles, compliance assistance centers, and more.

Combustion Portal: compliance assistance center.

Enforcement

National Enforcement Initiatives_: Reducing Widespread Air Pollution from the Largest Sources, especially the Coal-Fired Utility, Cement, Glass, and Acid Sectors_

Policies and Guidance

Compliance Assistance: _Chemical Sector Guidance Documents_

Compliance Guidance for Industrial Process Refrigeration Leak Repairs Regulations Under Section 608 Clean Air Act (PDF) (59 pp)

Related Technical Information

AP 42 - Chapter 6: Organic Chemical Process Industry and _Chapter 8: Inorganic Chemical Industry:_ emission factors and process information for air pollution source categories.

<ins>_Computer and Electronic Product Manufacturing_</ins>

Laws and Regulations

National Emissions Standards for Hazardous Air Pollutants (NESHAP): air toxics regulations:

Degreasing Organic Cleaners (Halogenated Solvent Cleaners)

Magnetic Tape (surface coating)

Semiconductor Manufacturing

Stratospheric Ozone Regulations:

The Phaseout of Ozone Depleting Substances

Significant New Alternatives Policy (SNAP) Program: EPA's program to evaluate and regulate substitutes for the ozone-depleting chemicals that are being phased out under the stratospheric ozone protection provisions of the Clean Air Act (CAA).

Compliance

Computer/Electronics Sector Compliance Assistance: including industry profiles, compliance assistance centers, and more.

Policies and Guidance

Protocol for Conducting Environmental Compliance, Audits of Treatment, Storage and Disposal Facilities under the Resource Conservation and Recovery Act (PDF) (246 pp, 712 K)

Food Processing
Laws and Regulations

Air:

National Emissions Standards for Hazardous Air Pollutants (NESHAP): air toxics regulations:

Commercial Sterilizers

Industrial, Commercial and Institutional Boilers and Process Heaters

Manufacturing of Nutritional Yeast

Vegetable Oil Production; Solvent Extraction

Pesticides:

Implementation of Requirments under the Food Quality Protection Act (FQPA)

Pesticide Tolerances

Tolerances and Exemptions for Pesticide Chemical Residues in Food: 40 CFR Part 180, from the GPO's electronic CFR (e-CFR)

Water:

Effluent Guidelines: Meat and Poultry Products

Compliance

Combustion Portal: compliance assistance center.

Food Processing Sector Compliance Assistance: including sector profiles, compliance assistance centers, and more.

Related Technical Information

AP 42 - Chapter 9: Food and Agricultural Industries: emission factors and process information for air pollution source categories.

Furniture Manufacturing
Laws and Regulations

Formaldehyde Emissions from Pressed Wood Products

National Emission Standards for Hazardous Air Pollutants (NESHAP):

Metal Furniture (surface coating)

Wood Furniture (surface coating)

Significant New Alternatives Policy (SNAP) Program: EPA's program to evaluate and regulate substitutes for the ozone-depleting chemicals that are being phased out under the stratospheric ozone protection provisions of the Clean Air Act (CAA).

Compliance

Furniture Sector Compliance Assistance: including sector profiles and compliance assistance sectors.

RCRA in Focus: Furniture Manufacturing and Refinishing (PDF) (16 pp, 329K): A guide for small business, includes a hazardous waste table of RCRA requirements and answers to frequently asked questions.

Related Technical Information

AP 42 - Chapter 10: Wood Products Industry: emission factors and process information for air pollution source categories.

Metals:

Laws and Regulations

Air:

National Emission Standards for Hazardous Air Pollutants (NESHAP):

Benzene Waste Operations

Chromium Electroplating

Coke Ovens: Pushing, Quenching,& Battery Stacks

Coke Ovens (Charging, Top Side, and Door Leaks)

Degreasing Organic Cleaners (Halogenated Solvent Cleaners)

Electric Arc Furnace Steelmaking Facilities (Area Sources)

Ferromanganese and Silicomanganese Production (Ferroalloys, Major Sources)

Industrial Cooling Towers

Integrated Iron and Steel

Iron and Steel Foundries (Major Sources)

Lime Manufacturing

Metal Can (surface coating)

Metal Coil (surface coating)

Metal Furniture (surface coating)

Paper and Other Web (surface coating)

Polyvinyl Chloride and Copolymers Production

Primary Aluminum

Primary Copper

Primary Lead Smelting

Primary Magnesium Refining

Reinforced Plastic Composites Production

Secondary Aluminum

Secondary Lead Smelters

Water:

Iron and Steel Rulemaking Process: effluent guidelines.

Metal Products and Machinery: effluent guidelines.

Compliance

Combustion Portal: compliance assistance center.

Industrial Materials Recycling: Foundry Sand

Metals Sector Compliance Assistance: including sector profiles and assistance centers.

Mining and Mineral Processing Compliance Assistance Resources for the Gold and Copper Industries (PDF) (19 pp, 703 K)

Related Technical Information

AP 42 - Chapter 12: Metallurgical Industry - emission factors and process information for air pollution source categories.

<u>Mineral Processing</u>

Laws and Regulations

Air:

National Emission Standards for Hazardous Air Pollutants (NESHAP): air toxics regulations:

Asbestos

Friction Products Manufacturing

Hazardous Waste Combustion

Industrial, Commercial and Institutional Boilers and Process Heaters

Industrial Cooling Towers

Lime Manufacturing

Mineral Wool Production

Paper and Other Web (surface coating)

Portland Cement Manufacturing

Refractory Products Manufacturing

Reinforced Plastic Composites Production

Wet Formed Fiberglass Mat Production

Wool Fiberglass Manufacturing

Asbestos:

Asbestos Laws and Regulations

Waste:

> *Industrial Waste: Mineral Processing Waste*
>
> **Water:**
>
> National Pollutant Discharge Elimination System (NPDES): *wastewater permit information.*
>
> > *Industrial and Commercial Facilities*
> >
> > *NPDES Stormwater Program: Industrial Activities*

Compliance

> *Combustion Portal: compliance assistance center.*
>
> *Compliance Assistance: Mineral Processing Wastes*
>
> *Compliance Assistance: Read Mixed Concrete, Crushed Stone, Sand, and Gravel*
>
> *Industrial Stormwater*
>
> *Minerals/Mining/Processing Sector Compliance Assistance: including sector profiles and assistance centers.*

Enforcement

> *Reducing Pollution from Mineral Processing Operations:* National enforcement initiatives

Related Business Sectors

> *Metals*
>
> *Mining (except oil and gas)*

Related Technical Information

> *AP 42 - Chapter 11: Mineral Products Industry:* emission factors and process information for air pollution source categories.

Petroleum

Laws and Regulations

> **Air:**
>
> National Emission Standards for Hazardous Air Pollutants (NESHAP):
>
> > *Asphalt Processing and Asphalt Roofing Manufacturing*
> >
> > *Benzene Waste Operations*
> >
> > *Coke Ovens: Pushing, Quenching,& Battery Stacks*
> >
> > *Coke Ovens* (Charging, Top Side, and Door Leaks)
> >
> > *Gasoline Dispensing and Distribution (Area and Major Sources)*
> >
> > *Hazardous Waste Combustion*
> >
> > *Industrial Cooling Towers*
> >
> > *Organic Liquids Distribution* (non-gasoline)
> >
> > *Petroleum Refineries*

Petroleum Refineries (Catalytic Cracking, Catalytic Reforming, Sulfur Plant Units, Associated Bypass Lines)
Site Remediation

Emergencies:

Discharge of Oil Regulation Overview: also known as the "sheen rule." Framework for determining whether an oil spill to inland and coastal waters and/or their adjoining shorelines should be reported to the federal government.

Oil Pollution Act Overview

Oil Pollution Prevention Regulation Overview

Oil Program: Laws and Regulations: EPA's emergency response program for health and environmental threats posed by inadvertent releases of oil and hazardous substances

SPCC Rule: includes requirements for oil spill prevention, preparedness, and response to prevent oil discharges to navigable waters and adjoining shorelines.

Water:

Effluent Guidelines for Oil and Gas Extraction (Synthetic-Based Drilling Fluids)

Compliance

Combustion Portal: compliance assistance center.

Petroleum Sector Compliance Assistance: sector profiles and assistance centers.

Enforcement

Clean Air Act National Enforcement Initiative: Fuels Enforcement: includes all parties in the fuel distribution system, including refiners.

Petroleum Refinery National Initiative Case Results

Policies and Guidance

Benzene National Emission Standards for Hazardous Air Pollutants (NESHAP) Frequently Ask Questions (FAQ) Handbook for Subparts FF and BB (PDF) (44 pp, 269 K)

Emergency Management: Policy & Guidance: includes guidance on the Spill Prevention Control and Countermeasure (SPCC) Rule

Petroleum Refining Maximum Achievable Control Technology (MACT) Standard Enabling Document (PDF) (125 pp, 1094 K)

Related Business Sectors

Oil and Gas Extraction Sector

Related Technical Information

AP 42 - Chapter 5: Petroleum Industry: emission factors and process information for air pollution source categories.

Pharmaceutical and Medicine Manufacturing
Laws and Regulations

Air:

> Essential Uses of CFCs for Metered-Dose Inhalers:
>
> National Emissions Standards for Hazardous Air Pollutants (NESHAP): Pharmaceutical Production Industry

General:

> Inorganic Chemical Manufacturing Statutory and Regulatory Summaries (PDF) (191 pp)

Waste:

> Universal Wastes: Pharmaceuticals

Water:

> Effluent Guidelines: Pharmaceutical Manufacturing

Compliance

Air:

> Compliance Assistance Tool for Clean Air Act Regulations: Subpart GGG of 40 CFR NESHAPS for Source Category Pharmaceutical Production (PDF) (260 pp, 7066 K)
>
> Compliance Assistance Tool for Pharmaceutical Production, Pesticide Active Ingredient Production, and Miscellaneous Organic Chemical Manufacturing NESHAP: Comparison of Regulatory Requirements and Case Study Compliance Illustrations for Nondedicated Equipment (PDF) (85 pp, 1505 K)
>
> Responsible Practices: Servicing and Disposing of Refrigeration Equipment (PDF) (2 pp)

General:

> EPA/CMA Root Cause Analysis Pilot Project: An Industrial Survey: EPA and the Chemical Manufacturing Association (CMA) report on the underlying causes of environmental violations.
>
> Pharmaceuticals Sector Compliance Assistance: including sector profiles and assistance centers.

Waste:

> Process-Based Self-Assessment Tool for the Organic Chemical Industry (PDF) (408 pp)

Policies and Guidance

> Compliance Guidance for Industrial ProceRefrigeration Leak Repairs Regulations Under Section 608 Clean Air Act (PDF) (59 pp)

<u>Chemical Industry Compliance Improvement Tool (CIT)</u>
<u>Chemical Industry National Environmental Baseline Report 1990-1994</u>

Related Business Sector

<u>Chemical Manufacturing</u>

Plastics and Rubber Products Manufacturing

Laws and Regulations

- *Air:*

  National Emission Standards for Hazardous Air Pollutants (NESHAP):

  <u>Cellulose Products Manufacturing</u>
  <u>Fabric Printing, Coating & Dyeing</u>
  <u>Flexible Polyurethane Foam Fabrication Operation</u>
  <u>Industrial Cooling Towers</u>
  <u>Metal Coil</u> (surface coating)
  <u>Paper and Other Web</u> (surface coating)
  <u>Printing and Publishing</u> (surface coating)
  <u>Reinforced Plastic Composites Production</u>
  <u>Rubber Tire Manufacturing</u>

- *Water:*

  <u>Effluent Guidelines: Organic Chemicals, Plastics and Synthetic Fibers (OCPSF)</u>

Compliance

- <u>Combustion Portal:</u> compliance assistance   center.
  <u>Rubber, Plastic and Man-made Fiber Sector Compliance Assistance:</u> sector profiles and assistance centers.

Related Technical Information

<u>AP 42 - Chapter 6: Organic Chemical Process Industry:</u> emission factors and process information for air pollution source categories, including the plastics industry.

Printing and Related Support Activities

Laws and Regulations

<u>Federal Environmental Regulations Potentially Affecting the Commercial Printing Industry (PDF)</u> (76 pp, 171 K)

National Emissions Standards for Hazardous Air Pollutants (NESHAP): air toxics regulations:

> Metal Coil (surface coating)
>
> Paper and Other Web (surface coating)
>
> Plastic Parts (surface coating)
>
> Printing and Publishing (surface coating)

Compliance

> Printing Sector Compliance Assistance: including sector profiles and assistance centers.
>
> RCRA in Focus: Printing (PDF) (15 pp, 245 K): A guide for small business, includes a hazardous waste table of RCRA requirements and answers frequently asked questions.

Policies and Guidance

> Multimedia Compliance/Pollution Prevention Assessment Guidance for Lithographic Printing Facilities (PDF) (91 pp)
>
> Multimedia Compliance Pollution Prevention Assessment Guidance for Screen Printing Facilities (PDF) (110 pp)

Related Technical Information

> AP 42 - Chapter 6: Organic Chemical Process Industry: emission factors and process information for air pollution source categories, including printing ink.

Shipbuilding (Transportation Equipment Manufacturing)

Laws and Regulations

> National Emission Standards for Hazardous Air Pollutants (NESHAP): air toxics regulations:
>
> > Auto & Light Duty Truck (surface coating)
> >
> > Boat Manufacturing
> >
> > Degreasing Organic Cleaners (Halogenated Solvent Cleaners)
> >
> > Engine Test Cells/Stands (Combined with Rocket Testing Facilities)
> >
> > Friction Products Manufacturing
> >
> > Metal Coil (surface coating)
> >
> > Plastic Parts (surface coating)
> >
> > Reinforced Plastic Composites Production
> >
> > Shipbuilding & Ship Repair (surface coating)

Nonroad Engines, Equipment and Vehicles:
> *Diesel Boats and Ships*
> *Gasoline Boats and Personal Watercraft*
> *Ocean Vessels and Large Ships*

Compliance

Combustion Portal: compliance assistance center.

Shipbuilding and Repair Sector Compliance Assistance: including sector profiles and assistance centers.

Policy and Guidance

Managing Used Oil: Advice for Small Business: used oil management standards.

Polluted Runoff: Marinas and Boating: managing nonpoint source pollution from marinas and recreational boating activities.

Related Business Sector

Transportation

Textile Manufacturing

Laws and Regulations

National Emissions Standards for Hazardous Air Pollutants (NESHAP):
> *Fabric Printing, Coating & Dyeing*
> *Industrial Cooling Towers*
> *Leather Tanning and Finishing Operations*

Compliance

Textile Sector Compliance Assistance: including sector profiles and assistance centers.

RCRA in Focus: Textile Manufacturing (PDF) (15 pp, 503K) *A guide for small business, includes a hazardous waste table of RCRA requirements and answers to frequently asked questions.*

RCRA in Focus: Leather Manufacturing (PDF) (20 pp, 359K): *A guide for small business, includes a hazardous waste table of RCRA requirements and answers to frequently asked questions.*

Policies and Guidance

Guidance Manual for Leather Tanning and Finishing Pretreatment Standards

Related Business Sector

Dry Cleaning Sector

Wood Product Manufacturing and Paper Manufacturing

Laws and Regulations

Air:

National Emission Standards for Hazardous Air Pollutants (NESHAP):

Industrial, Commercial and Institutional Boilers and Process Heaters

Magnetic Tape (surface coating)

Misc. Metal Parts and Products (surface coating)

Paper and Other Web (surface coating)

Plywood and Composite Wood Products (formerly Plywood and Particle Board Manufacturing)

Printing and Publishing (surface coating)

Pulp & Paper (non-combust) MACT

Wood Building Products (surface coating, formerly Flat Wood Paneling Products)

Water:

Effluent Guidelines: Pulp and Paper Rulemaking Actions: The water portion of the Pulp and Paper Cluster Rule. The other portion of the Cluster Rule is the air toxics rule, Pulp and Paper Production MACT.

Compliance

Combustion Portal: compliance assistance center.

Printing Sector Compliance Assistance: including sector profiles and assistance centers.

Pulp/Paper/Lumber Sector Compliance Assistance

Policies and Guidance

Wood Preserving Resource Conservation and Recovery Act Compliance Guide (PDF) (117 pp)

Kraft Pulp Mill Compliance Assessment Guide (PDF) (357 pp)

Mining (except Oil and Gas)

Laws and Regulations

Air:

National Emissions Standards for Hazardous Air Pollutants (NESHAP): air toxics regulations:

Gold Mine Ore Processing and Production (Area Sources)

Taconite Iron Ore Processing

Radiation Protection, including uranium mining and mill tailings

Asbestos:

Asbestos Laws and Regulations

Waste:

Industrial Waste: Mining Waste

TENORM: Mining Wastes: information about Technologically-Enhanced, Naturally-Occurring Radioactive Material (TENORM) produced from mining wastes.

Water:

Effluent Guidelines: Coal Mining Point Source Category

Mid-Atlantic Mountaintop Mining: information about mountaintop coal mining and surface mining.

National Pollutant Discharge Elimination System (NPDES): wastewater permits:

Mining

Stormwater Discharges from Industrial Facilities

Surface Coal Mining Activities under the Clean Water Act Section 404: wetlands regulations affecting mining activities.

Underground Injection Control (UIC) Regulations

Compliance

Minerals/Mining/Processing Sector Compliance Assistance: including sector profiles and assistance centers.

Enforcement

National Enforcement Initiatives: Mineral Processing

Policies and Guidance

Wetlands Policy & Guidance: Surface Coal Mining Activities under Clean Water Act Section 404

Polluted Runoff: Acid Mine Drainage: includes guidance documents for characterizing and cleaning up abandoned mine sites.

Abandoned Mine Land: Policy and Guidance: Part of EPA's Superfund program, includes policy and guidance documents that have direct applications to the assessment and remediation of abandoned mine lands.

Related Business Sectors

Metals

Mineral Processing

Oil and Gas Extraction
Laws and Regulations
Air:
National Emissions Standards for Hazardous Air Pollutants (NESHAP):
>> *Oil & Natural Gas Production (includes Area Sources)*
>> *Reciprocating Internal Combustion Engines (RICE), including area sources*
>> *Stationary Combustion Turbines*

Waste:
> *Industrial Waste: Crude Oil and Natural Gas Waste*

Water:
> *Effluent Guidelines: Oil and Gas Extraction (Synthetic-Based Drilling Fluids)*
> *Underground Injection Control (UIC) Regulations*

Compliance
Petroleum Sector Compliance Assistance: including sector profiles and assistance centers.

Enforcement
National Enforcement Initiatives*: Assuring energy extraction sector compliance with environmental laws*

Related Business Sectors
Petroleum Manufacturing

American Indian and Alaska Native Tribal Governments
Laws and Regulations
American Indian Tribal Portal: Laws & Regulations
National Emissions Standards for Hazardous Air Pollutants (NESHAPS): *air toxics regulations:*
> *Industrial, Commercial and Institutional Boilers and Process Heaters*
> *Municipal Solid Waste Landfills*

Compliance

Combustion Portal: compliance assistance center.

Tribal Sector Compliance Assistance: including sector profiles and assistance centers.

TSCA Section 402/404: Lead-Based Paint Renovation Program (PDF) (122 pp, 257 K): guidance to assist states and tribes to manage lead renovation, repair and painting programs.

Enforcement

National Enforcement Initiative: Indian Country

Federal Facilities

Laws and Regulations

Federal Facilities Restoration and Reuse: base closures and transfers, hazardous waste, military munitions, perchorlate, and other regulatory information.

National Emissions Standards for Hazardous Air Pollutants (NESHAPS): air toxics regulations:

    Industrial, Commercial and Institutional Boilers and Process Heaters

    Municipal Solid Waste Landfills

Radiation Cleanup and Multi-Agency Programs

Compliance

Combustion Portal: compliance assistance center.

Comprehensive Procurement Guideline: purchasing products with recycled or recovered materials.

Environmentally Preferable Purchasing (EPP): helps the federal government "buy green."

Federal Facilities Sector Compliance Assistance: including sector profiles and assistance centers.

Enforcement

Federal Facilities Enforcement

Policies and Guidance

Federal Facilities enforcement policies

Federal Facilities publications

International Affairs

Laws and Regulations

Air:

Montreal Protocol on Substances that Deplete the Ozone Layer: This treaty is the basis on which *Title VI of the Clean Air Act* was established.

National Emissions Standards for Hazardous Air Pollutants (NESHAPS):

Industrial, Commercial and Institutional Boilers and Process Heaters

Municipal Solid Waste Landfills

Reciprocating Internal Combustion Engines (RICE), including area sources

General:

International Programs – Information about bilateral programs with key partner countries, trade agreements, treaties and more.

Pesticides:

Regulating Pesticides: International Issues

Toxic Substances:

Pollution Prevention and Toxics: International Activities: harmonization and test guidelines, chemical substance exports, and persistent organic pollutant negotiations.

Waste:

International Waste Agreements: Waste agreements between the US and foreign countries.

Water:

Great Lakes Water Quality Agreement: Rights and obligations of Canada and the United States under the Great Lakes Water Quality Agreement.

International Convention for the Prevention of Pollution from Ships (MARPOL 73/78): International treaty regulating the disposal of wastes generated by normal operation of vessels.

Compliance

Border Compliance Assistance Center: transporting solid and hazardous wastes from Mexico into the United States.

Combustion Portal: compliance assistance center.

International Import and Export: including chemical substances, pesticides, and hazardous wastes.

Port Compliance _ compliance assistance center

Enforcement

Enforcing vehicle and engine certification on imported vehicles

Local Governments

Laws and Regulations

Air

National Emission Standards for Hazardous Air Pollutants (NESHAP): air toxics regulations:

> Industrial, Commercial and Institutional Boilers and Process Heaters
> Publicly Owned Treatment Works (POTWs)
> Municipal Solid Waste Landfill
> State Implementation Plans Status and Information: how states and EPA work together to meet and maintain National Ambient Air Quality Standards.

Emergencies

> Emergency Planning and Community Right-to-Know (EPCRA) Local Emergency Planning Requirements

Water

Effluent Guidelines: Drinking Water Treatment: to address the direct discharge of drinking water treatment residuals to surface water, together with the indirect discharge of residuals to wastewater treatment plants.

National Pollutant Discharge Elimination System (NPDES): wastewater permitting:

> Municipalities and Wastewater Treatment Plants: includes stormwater and sewer overflow information.

Public Drinking Water Systems Programs

Water Security: Legislation and Directives: protecting water supply and utilities

Compliance

Combustion Portal: compliance assistance center.

Compliance Guidance under the Safe Drinking Water Act: information for public drinking water systems

Local Government Compliance Assistance: including sector profiles and compliance assistance centers.

Small Communities Compliance and Enforcement

TSCA Section 402/404: Lead-Based Paint Renovation Program (PDF) (122 pp, 257 K): guidance to assist states and tribes to manage lead renovation, repair and painting programs.

Wastewater in Small Communities: financial, technical, and programmatic assistance.

Enforcement

Cleanup Enforcement: State and Local Government Activities and Liability Protections

Automotive Repair and Maintenance

Laws and Regulations

Motor Vehicle Air Conditioning (Servicing): refrigerant service and handling for motor vehicles.

National Emissions Standards for Hazardous Air Pollutants (NESHAP): air toxics regulations:

Automobile & Light Duty Truck Surface Coating

Engine Test Cells/Stands (Combined with Rocket Testing Facilities)

Paint Stripping and Miscellaneous Surface Coating Operations (PDF) (2 pp): brochure   for   area   sources

Transportation and Air Quality: information about on-road and nonroad vehicles, engines, equipment, fuels and fuel additives. Including:

Engine Testing Regulations, including 40 CFR 1065.

Fuel and Fuel Additives: Registration

On-Board Diagnostics: Repair Technicians: information for service and repair technicians

On-Road Vehicles and Engines: cars, light trucks, and highway vehicles

Mobile Sources Air Toxics: Regulations

Compliance

Automotive Sector Compliance Assistance: including sector profiles and assistance centers.

RCRA in Focus: Vehicle Maintenance (PDF) (20 pp, 371K): A guide for small business, includes a hazardous waste table of RCRA requirements and answers to frequently asked questions.

Enforcement

Clean Air Act National Enforcement Initiatives: Mobile Source Enforcement: Including heavy duty engines, fuels, defeat devices, and on-board diagnostics.

Policies and Guidance

Managing Used Oil: Advice for Small Businesses - used oil management standards.

Related Business Sector

Transportation

Dry Cleaning

Laws and Regulations

National Emissions Standards for Hazardous Air Pollutants (NESHAP): Perchloroethylene Dry Cleaning Facilities

Compliance

Dry Cleaning Sector Compliance Assistance: including sector profiles and assistance centers.

RCRA in Focus: Dry Cleaning (PDF) (20 pp, 548 K): a guide for small business, includes a hazardous waste table of RCRA requirements.

Policies and Guidance

Multimedia Inspection Checklist for Dry Cleaning Facilities (PDF) (13 pp)

Plain English Guide for Perc Cleaners

Protocols for Conducting Environmental Compliance Audits under the Emergency Planning and Community Right-to-Know Act (PDF) (63 pp, 358 K)

Protocol for Conducting Environmental Compliance, Audits of Hazardous Waste Generators under the Resource Conservation and Recovery Act (PDF) (178 pp, 729 K)

Retail Trade

Laws and Regulations

National Emissions Standards for Hazardous Air Pollutants (NESHAP): Gasoline Dispensing and Distribution (Area and Major Sources)

Compliance

Retail Industry Portal - programs and resources available to help prevent and resolve environmental issues at retail establishments.

Retail: Compliance Overview

Enforcement

Enforcing vehicle and engine certification on imported vehicles

Transportation

Laws and Regulations

Air:

National Emissions Standards for Hazardous Air Pollutants (NESHAP): air toxics regulations:

> *Engine Test Cells/Stands* (Combined with Rocket Testing Facilities)
> *Gasoline Dispensing and Distribution (Area and Major Sources)*
> *Organic Liquids Distribution* (non-gasoline)
> *Reciprocating Internal Combustion Engines (RICE)*, including area sources
> *Transportation and Air Quality:* information about on-road and nonroad vehicles, engines, equipment, fuels and fuel additives. Including:
> *Aircraft*
> *Diesel Boats and Ships*
> *Locomotives*

Water:

> *Effluent Guidelines: Transportation Equipment Cleaning*
> National Pollutant Discharge Elimination System (NPDES): wastewater permit information:
> > *Vessel Discharges*
> > *Pressure Wash/ Power Wash Discharges*
> > *Vessel Sewage Discharges and No Discharge Zones*

Compliance

Border Compliance Assistance Center: http://www.epa.gov/epahome/exitepa.htm information about transporting solid and hazardous wastes from Mexico into the United States
International Import and Export: including chemical substances, pesticides, and hazardous wastes.
Port Compliance compliance assistance center
Transportation Sector Compliance Assistance: includes sector profiles and assistance centers.

Policies and Guidance

Environmental Screening Checklist and Workbook for Trucking Industry
Polluted Runoff: Roads, Highways and Bridges: includes guidance for managing nonpoint source pollution from transportation infrastructure.

Related Business Sectors

Aerospace Sector
Automotive Sector
Shipbuilding Sector

Electric Power Generation, Transmission and Distribution

Laws and Regulations

Air:

Controlling Power Plant Emissions: Overview: information about controlling mercury and other hazardous air pollutants from power plants.

Cross-State Air Pollution Rule (CSAPR): Requires 27 states to significantly improve air quality by reducing power plant emissions that contribute to ozone and/or fine particle pollution in other states.

National Emissions Standards for Hazardous Air Pollutants (NESHAP): air toxics regulations:

Air Toxics Standards for Utilities

Benzene Waste Operations

Reciprocating Internal Combustion Engines (RICE), including area sources

Stationary Combustion Turbines

Utility NESHAP

Reducing Toxic Air Emissions from Power Plants: Regulatory Actions

General:

Energy Portal: Regulations and Standards: EPA's key energy-related regulations.

Waste:

Industrial Waste: Fossil Fuel Combustion Waste

Water:

Cooling Water Intake Structures: CWA §316(b): Final rules, court proceedings, and other documents related to the National Pollutant Discharge Elimination System (NPDES) rules for cooling water intake structures.

Compliance

Combustion Portal: compliance assistance center.

Industrial Materials Recycling: Coal Combustion Products

Power Generators Compliance Assistance: including sector profiles and assistance centers.

Enforcement

Coal-Fired Power Plant Enforcement Initiative

National Enforcement Initiatives: *Assuring Energy Extraction Sector Compliance with Environmental Laws*

National Enforcement Initiatives: *Reducing Widespread Air Pollution from the Largest Sources, especially the Coal-Fired Utility, Cement, Glass, and Acid Sectors*

OH, MY!

As you can see, there isn't a single part of our lives that is not controlled, regulated or otherwise hampered by the EPA. It is as if the agency were begging "Feed Me! Feed Me!"

There's no way to tone it down. No way to try to bring it back to reality. No way to convince people that the EPA's is out of control. So what's the answer?

<u>GET RID OF THE EPA!</u> – It is time to close shop and send everyone home and start from scratch.

Start from scratch with a new, simple, concise Environmental Protection Administration or better yet, why not form a new agency and call it something else. What about: **"The United States Department of Common Sense and Living Good!"**
  This is a bit wordy but hey, it would be a new start.
  Why not turn jurisdiction and monitoring over to each state with certain general guidelines like: Common Sense!?

Wow! Can we do that?

Of course we can. It just takes the gumption, fortitude and courage to put everything back in line and let communal sense prevail.

(Note: We did not want to end this book with such a sour note as explaining the EPA, so we decided to move a couple chapters to the end, which will give you optimism to our future and a way that we can improve our lives better than ever and not at the expense of others. Please read on to Chapters 20 & 21.)

CHAPTER 20

Transportation – Erection when it counts.

We have outgrown our transportation system here in the United States by a mile. The transportation matrix is a huge problem to control, with such vast numbers and varieties of vehicles that we have, we must employ drastic, yet imaginative, new-age ideas.

Traffic will NOT get better. We can continue to build more and more two-, three-, four- and six-lane highways, but the volume of vehicles on our streets and highways will continue to grow exponentially. Automobile factories will continue to build vehicles and consumers will replace the old with the new. The growth problem in the United States is clearly demonstrated not only on the roads, but also in junk yards, demolition yards, and by those unsavory old, rusted vehicles parked here and there on local roads and back alleys and in some cases, in front of houses, like mine.

But what about Florida, Texas, California, and Hawaii, among a number of other states, where nothing is close together? In states such as these, cities and towns are miles apart from each other and public transportation is almost non-existent.

In California City, CA, the small town of about 12,000 people where I live, the market is about three miles from the house. In this desert city, a vehicle is required just to shop at the only market, visit a friend on the other side of town or to go to work (though jobs are hard to come by in Cal-City). Vehicle transportation is essential.

Add the costs of vehicle ownership, registration, insurance and fuel together and what you have is a society deeply trapped by its need for transportation. Most folks are simply without other options.

A NEW APPROACH TO TRANSPORTATION – Let's start with our crowded freeway systems.

In many parts of the country we need more lanes added to our highways to improve traffic flow. Admittedly, obtaining the right-a-way to add lanes to existing freeways or to build entirely new roads seems nearly impossible. It takes years to go over all the hurdles, not the least of which is that the same people who complain about traffic also do not want to build anything that will disrupt their neighborhood or way of living. "Build it somewhere else, but not around here," is often the appeal heard at municipal meetings.

Then there are the "Eco-freaks" who object to everything with the same excuse, "We're trying to save our environment, our planet." Whether or not these folks understand the impact of proposed initiatives is unclear; they just default to their position. That's hog-wash!

Some cities in the United States have added freeway lanes above existing ones. This can be a good solution, but really is not practical for most places as it disturbs traffic for ten to twenty years before the project is completed.

Instead of building new highways or purchasing new land, we already have easements in place for our freeways and expressways. These "easements" are already paid for!

So the solution lies in what we can do to improve what we already have!

The "Erector Set" method of building is the answer. These ideas may sound too simplistic and some will even think that I have taken too many things for granted; but, as I said before the KISS method is really the best approach to any problem or challenge. So here it goes:

PHASE ONE -

1. Choose either the center median or each side of any freeway or expressway. Erect steel towers high enough so as to not disturb existing traffic flow.
2. With the ever-improving GPS systems we now enjoy, calculate every inch of the median to record the absolute and correct elevations from one end of the project to the other.

3. Pre-fabricate steel bases to fit every section that will be used, as determined by the engineering. Make each base identical.

4. Pre-fabricate steel towers that will fit into every base and number them accordingly; always maintaining the same elevations, unless a change is needed for curves, going over or under bridges or other terrain variances.

5. Pre-fabricate either "mono-rails" or multiple rails (as per engineering) and hang those to the towers.

6. Below the rails add "catch" steel nets that will prevent any material to filter through to the existing right-of-way below.

7. Build either multi-passenger trains or individual pods or both to ride on those rails at prescribed speeds and times. These can incorporate the new "Mag-Lev" technology which uses magnets to move.

8. All components, including "passenger stations" and "emergency exits" will also be constructed under the "Erector Set" principle.

9. When all these components have been built, checked, doubled-checked and deemed one hundred percent construction worthy; then it is time to begin the job.

10. Close the outer lane (sometimes known as the "Diamond Lane," in each direction of the freeway or expressway, by using cement barriers with elevated partitions so that "lookie-loo's" don't slow down to see what's going on.

THE CONSTRUCTION PROCESS

PHASE ONE

First, a massive hole-digger follows the exact GPS coordinates and begins to bore the correct holes into the ground; normally straddling the center dividers. According to engineering specifications, these holes may be ten, twenty, thirty or even fifty-feet apart.

Following the "hole-digger" unit, heavy trucks designed to carry out the excess dirt or material from the ground can efficiently travel in the opposite direction.

At the same time, just behind the "hole-digger," the "Concrete Monster" cement source rig fills each hole with the exact amount of cement and compacts it. This massive unit pours over thousands of cubic yards of cement in a day. It is self-loading and mixing and can be replenished as needed

Behind the "Concrete Monster" runs the "Base Master" rig which systematically places each identical base at the exact location and height. All this is computerized for accuracy.

Once the bases have had the time to "set" and harden, a new GPS reading is taken to ensure that the location, height and placement are as prescribed. If there is a variance, slight or otherwise, these can be corrected with steel plates to adjust for height.

Engineering can determine the time needed before each concrete base is "set" and ready to absorb the weight of the tower and rails.

All the while traffic has only been disturbed by the closure of one lane on each side; something that happens all the time now-a-days for regular maintenance.

I estimate that a crew with the proper equipment for such a job can complete a mile a day from start to finish.

End of phase one.

PHASE TWO - Assembling the ERECTOR Set:

This is where the fun begins! A core of engineers, administrators, supervisors and crews with the precise equipment, can breeze through this at a rate of as much as a mile or two per day! Don't think so?

Let me show you how it can be done:

1. Remember, everything has already been pre-fabricated to exact dimensions for each section; including elevation changes, angles, curves, etc.
2. As the bases are deemed ready, the first piece of massive equipment; the mobile "Tower Anchor" rig straddles the median and begins to erect each tower to its corresponding base. This same piece of equipment will also anchor, set and bolt the tower using special tools designed specifically for this type of job.

3. Following the "Tower Anchor" rig, custom built "Rail Rack" carriers, one on each side, begin placing pieces of rails and "catch steel nets" to the towers. This is all automated and directed by engineers.

4. As sections of rails are completed, a final unit, the "Mother Load" begins to place "rail trains" atop each section of rail to test its strength, and match the parameters that have been engineered into the system. Weight, tension and tensile strength are all computer-monitored for accuracy and integrity. Changes can be made if a section does not meet the criteria.

5. While all this is happening, other crews are working between exit stations, drop-off venues and emergency exits along the freeway. Every expressway is built with areas next to bridges and underpasses which have nothing on them. They are "dead spots" that could be used for these purposes.

6. For those cities who wish to make these structures more appealing, light weight shells may be wrapped around each tower and under the rails in color coordinated motif's that can sport signs or advertising space. This technology is already being applied to large windmill blades and oil rigs.

7. The important thing to remember is that every facet of this project; including stations, exit spots, interchanges and monitor posts, are all constructed with steel and concrete, and can be erected anywhere.

8. In six months, sixty to eighty miles of rails can be totally completed and in use.

Crazy? Think about it. With everything measured, GPS-located, pre-fabricated and assembled to exact dimensions, this is totally doable and within our current capabilities. Good, old-fashion American knowhow has done it always. IT CAN BE DONE FOLKS!

Residual benefits of such a project are huge for our country, our economy and our way of life.

- More jobs for people at all levels.
- More jobs for steel workers as the demand for steel sky-rockets to record-breaking levels.
- Our own U.S. steel companies and cement factories and distributors will benefit first, and construction suppliers of every kind will also thrive.
- If we cannot produce all the steel, parts or other materials, we can import from neighboring countries (i.e. Canada, Mexico, South America); thus keeping this side of the world healthier -- economically speaking.
- Fuel consumption will drop tremendously as folks shift to this less expensive mode of transportation.
- Shuttles will overcome the need for individual transportation and carry people to their specific work hub from transfer stations along the way.
- One of the largest benefits will be realized in the control of traffic. A great majority of heavy vehicles, such as trucks, motor homes and RV's will have more space to operate safely on the existing highways, freeways or expressways.

- How about the trillion dollars we currently send to foreign countries to purchase oil from them? A good portion of that would be saved and spent here in the United States. Our economy will be as healthy as it has ever been. These savings alone would pay for this national project ten times over!

It is not inconceivable that with such an automated, computerized, new-age techno-system, we could also build and offer "individual auto-pods" that could take our vehicles along the same rail system and drop-off at predetermined locations punched-in at the outset of the trip. This would all be incorporated into the system.

In my case, I can imagine rolling up with my vehicle to the California City, CA station, setting my trusty 1995 Jeep on the pod, and allowing it to carry me approximately 138 miles to Marina Del Rey to visit family. Instead of driving, I could spend two to two-and-a-half hours listening to music, reading a book, doing business or just relaxing while the rail does its thing. Impossible? Absolutely not!

Heck, we now have cars that parallel park themselves and talk to you regarding traffic, and tell you what you want to know!

In the final analysis we must do something as dramatic as what I'm suggesting so that its implementation will make a strong impact in this country for the good.

I truly believe that when you compute the costs for a national project such as this one, they will be much less than anticipated if the same principles that Henry Ford originally applied in the assembly-line method are implemented on a large scale.

Now doesn't that beat it all? Instead of cutting a check for $200.00 to each tax-paying citizen and calling it a "stimulus," we would be putting our money to work for the masses. In fact, the workforce will increase beyond expectations. Heck, we might even have to open up our country for a temporary foreign labor-force visa!

CHAPTER 21

NEW-FOUND & UNTAPPED SOURCE OF ENERGY –
And it was all in front of us.

Think about it. Of the fuel we use to power our vehicles, seven to ten-percent is actually used to move from one place to another, while the other ninety percent of energy is wasted; never to be recovered and used again. In other words, this potential energy "goes up in smoke" or in this case, ends up as smog or spewed bio-carbons.

Wouldn't it be wonderful if while we were traveling and using up fuel we could also be generating energy? It can be done, but no one has started the program.

Here are several suggestions on how we can put to good use the untapped energy that is currently being produced by our vehicles as they move down the road:

- Set up magnetic fields under each vehicle so that while moving, we are creating "pulsating energy" where magnetic sensors imbedded in the ground can transfer electrical currents to a central location. From there, this energy could feed the thousands of miles of "electrical grid" spanning our towns, cities and states.
- If you've ever had a flat tire on the freeway, you know firsthand that vehicles produce wind energy as they pass by at high speeds. So why not harness that wind to drive built-in turbines alongside of the freeway to capture wind energy? With today's technology, all it takes is three to four-miles-per-hour winds to generate electricity from a windmill. So what's the hold-up?
- Almost every vehicle has a roof, hood or trunk. Why not make those body parts solar-energy accumulators, so that every moving vehicle can also send an electrical pulse to electrical conduits in the ground and thus, feed collector stations that distribute power locally, state-wide or nationally?

If every vehicle on the road contributed to creating electricity, we would have little or no need for massive fossil-fuel-burning electrical generating plants throughout the United States.

If the suggestions made in Chapter 20 and 21 are applied together with those ideas presented earlier in this book, I believe that our fossil-fuel consumption would drop dramatically.

We would save at least 50% of the fossil fuel we are currently using every day! That means that the trillions of dollars we are spending and sending elsewhere in the world to purchase energy would remain here to build things (as suggested) and improve our lives.

Of course there will be a myriad of objections against implementing these simple solutions. First and foremost, oil companies and their lobbyists both here and abroad will go to work to shut-down these approaches. Losing at least 50% of their revenue from the United States would be significant, and the long-lasting "party-on-us" they have enjoyed for over a half a century, will be over. Oil companies must be pressed to use their resources to create new energy industries and participate in the new age of technology.

Undeniably foreign nations that depend on the U.S. for the major portion of their economy would also have to look elsewhere for their power sources. The party would be over for both the hosts and the invited guests, baby.

Politicians who have depended on oil money or upon major contributors from the oil-lobby will actually have to find ways to prove themselves to their constituents. And if the changes to our election system that I recommend in this book are made, they will just have to work for us for a change. What a novel idea.

It would be great to have no more taxes to pay, solve the illegal immigrant issues, streamline election matters, and clean up a sundry of other problems in this book. If we can do it, we would be "living large" in the greatest country in the world; The United States of America.

Is this a great country or what?

EPILOGUE ONE

It was worth the wait to write it.

I started to write this book and put these ideas together years ago. However, in recent months, and with the upcoming elections of 2012, it has been necessary to continue to update some of the subjects.

At some point however, it is time to say, "Stop! This book needs to get published...no more updates."

As a result, by the time you read this book, there may be a number of circumstances that have already changed or may not apply.

Even so, the central concept of this book is the **KISS** principle. Life has gotten too complicated because many of us have allowed it to, but no more! At least not by me. I'm at the age that I don't give a hoot's asteroid about being politically correct and trying to appease everyone. We must make changes right away or we are doomed to live with our own laziness and indifference.

I hope this book has offered ideas that you might consider exploring and putting to use.

Many will say these changes will never happen because they will not be accepted by big government. Of course not but we have to start somewhere. We must take that the first step and let the chips fall where they may. That's how everything in life starts.

I began this book with the preamble of our Constitution, because it is as good of a beginning as any I can think of. The framing of those words was something special and God-driven. We did it right.

But now we are on the verge of dismissing our Constitutional moorings because either of convenience or laziness.

I hope I have encouraged you to think about and dream of the possibilities even as you hold onto our foundation. I am not advocating for war or demonstrations or the imposition of arbitrary laws, because I don't need to. If we can solve the problems as I have outlined in this book, everything else will fall into place.

But it all starts from the top and moves to the lower rungs. That's why I've used the "pyramid" graphic on this book's cover.

And those are the facts, Jack!

EV

EPILOUGE TWO

Our Living Constitution
Study it

This section of the book is for convenient future reference. It will do a lot of good if from time to time you skimmed over our Constitution just to see what our forefathers did for us as they structured our great country. We should appreciate their effort and their guidance.

The framers were so wise, so intuitive and so wonderful that it is really hard to put into words my feelings about what these few men did for our country. I believe that the document they prepared was ordained by God in every detail.

The United States Constitution must be thought of as the greatest document ever to bless our land. It must be part of our daily lives. It must be constantly referenced, studied and taught to make sure that our nation is heading down the right path.

We can never take the Constitution for granted, leave it behind or dismiss it as if it was not relevant in today's society.

More than ever, we must be mindful that the Constitution is the cornerstone of our country and as such, we must never let it erode away or permit to be demolished. However, this "living" document must be amended from time-to-time to keep pace with our modern problems and progressive lives.

This is OUR CONSTITUTION. Please study it as one day it is likely that you will need to remember it!

Note: The text below is as it was originally written in 1778.

We the People of the United States, in Order to

form a more perfect Union, establish Justice, insure domestic Tranquility, provide for the common defence, promote the general Welfare, and secure the Blessings of Liberty to ourselves and our Posterity, do ordain and establish this Constitution for the United States of America..."

Article. I.

Section. 1.

All legislative Powers herein granted shall be vested in a Congress of the United States, which shall consist of a Senate and House of Representatives.

Section. 2.

The House of Representatives shall be composed of Members chosen every second Year by the People of the several States, and the Electors in each State shall have the Qualifications requisite for Electors of the most numerous Branch of the State Legislature.

No Person shall be a Representative who shall not have attained to the Age of twenty five Years, and been seven Years a Citizen of the United

States, and who shall not, when elected, be an Inhabitant of that State in which he shall be chosen.

Representatives and direct Taxes shall be apportioned among the several States which may be included within this Union, according to their respective Numbers, which shall be determined by adding to the whole Number of free Persons, including those bound to Service for a Term of Years, and excluding Indians not taxed, three fifths of all other Persons. The actual Enumeration shall be made within three Years after the first Meeting of the Congress of the United States, and within every subsequent Term of ten Years, in such Manner as they shall by Law direct. The Number of Representatives shall not exceed one for every thirty Thousand, but each State shall have at Least one Representative; and until such enumeration shall be made, the State of New Hampshire shall be entitled to chuse three, Massachusetts eight, Rhode-Island and Providence Plantations one, Connecticut five, New-York six, New Jersey four, Pennsylvania eight, Delaware one, Maryland six, Virginia ten, North Carolina five, South Carolina five, and Georgia three.

When vacancies happen in the Representation from any State, the Executive Authority thereof shall issue Writs of Election to fill such Vacancies.

The House of Representatives shall chuse their Speaker and other Officers; and shall have the sole Power of Impeachment.

Section. 3.

The Senate of the United States shall be composed of two Senators from each State, chosen by the Legislature thereof for six Years; and each Senator shall have one Vote.

Immediately after they shall be assembled in Consequence of the first Election, they shall be divided as equally as may be into three Classes. The Seats of the Senators of the first Class shall be vacated at the Expiration of the second Year, of the second Class at the Expiration of the fourth Year, and of the third Class at the Expiration of the sixth Year, so that one third may be chosen every second Year; and if Vacancies happen by Resignation, or otherwise, during the Recess of the Legislature of any State, the Executive thereof may make temporary Appointments until the next Meeting of the Legislature, which shall then fill such Vacancies.

No Person shall be a Senator who shall not have attained to the Age of thirty Years, and been nine Years a Citizen of the United States, and who shall not, when elected, be an Inhabitant of that State for which he shall be chosen.

The Vice President of the United States shall be President of the Senate, but shall have no Vote, unless they be equally divided.

The Senate shall chuse their other Officers, and also a President pro tempore, in the Absence of the Vice President, or when he shall exercise the Office of President of the United States.

The Senate shall have the sole Power to try all Impeachments. When sitting for that Purpose, they shall be on Oath or Affirmation. When the President of the United States is tried, the Chief Justice shall preside:

And no Person shall be convicted without the Concurrence of two thirds of the Members present.

Judgment in Cases of Impeachment shall not extend further than to removal from Office, and disqualification to hold and enjoy any Office of honor, Trust or Profit under the United States: but the Party convicted shall nevertheless be liable and subject to Indictment, Trial, Judgment and Punishment, according to Law.

Section. 4.

The Times, Places and Manner of holding Elections for Senators and Representatives, shall be prescribed in each State by the Legislature thereof; but the Congress may at any time by Law make or alter such Regulations, except as to the Places of chusing Senators.

The Congress shall assemble at least once in every Year, and such Meeting shall be on the first Monday in December, unless they shall by Law appoint a different Day.

Section. 5.

Each House shall be the Judge of the Elections, Returns and Qualifications of its own Members, and a Majority of each shall constitute a Quorum to do Business; but a smaller Number may adjourn from day to day, and may be authorized to compel the Attendance of absent Members, in such Manner, and under such Penalties as each House may provide.

Each House may determine the Rules of its Proceedings, punish its Members for disorderly Behaviour, and, with the Concurrence of two thirds, expel a Member.

Each House shall keep a Journal of its Proceedings, and from time to time publish the same, excepting such Parts as may in their Judgment require Secrecy; and the Yeas and Nays of the Members of either House on any question shall, at the Desire of one fifth of those Present, be entered on the Journal.

Neither House, during the Session of Congress, shall, without the Consent of the other, adjourn for more than three days, nor to any other Place than that in which the two Houses shall be sitting.

Section. 6.

The Senators and Representatives shall receive a Compensation for their Services, to be ascertained by Law, and paid out of the Treasury of the United States. They shall in all Cases, except Treason, Felony and Breach of the Peace, be privileged from Arrest during their Attendance at the Session of their respective Houses, and in going to and returning from the same; and for any Speech or Debate in either House, they shall not be questioned in any other Place.

No Senator or Representative shall, during the Time for which he was elected, be appointed to any civil Office under the Authority of the United States, which shall have been created, or the Emoluments whereof shall have been encreased during such time; and no Person holding any Office under the United States, shall be a Member of either House during his Continuance in Office.

Section. 7.

All Bills for raising Revenue shall originate in the House of Representatives; but the Senate may propose or concur with Amendments as on other Bills.

Every Bill which shall have passed the House of Representatives and the Senate, shall, before it become a Law, be presented to the President of the United States: If he approve he shall sign it, but if not he shall return it, with his Objections to that House in which it shall have originated, who shall enter the Objections at large on their Journal, and proceed to reconsider it. If after such Reconsideration two thirds of that House shall agree to pass the Bill, it shall be sent, together with the Objections, to the other House, by which it shall likewise be reconsidered, and if approved by two thirds of that House, it shall become a Law. But in all such Cases the Votes of both Houses shall be determined by yeas and Nays, and the Names of the Persons voting for and against the Bill shall be entered on the Journal of each House respectively. If any Bill shall not be returned by the President within ten Days (Sundays excepted) after it shall have been presented to him, the Same shall be a Law, in like Manner as if he had signed it, unless the Congress by their Adjournment prevent its Return, in which Case it shall not be a Law.

Every Order, Resolution, or Vote to which the Concurrence of the Senate and House of Representatives may be necessary (except on a question of Adjournment) shall be presented to the President of the United States; and before the Same shall take Effect, shall be approved by him, or being disapproved by him, shall be repassed by two thirds of the Senate and House of Representatives, according to the Rules and Limitations prescribed in the Case of a Bill.

Section. 8.

The Congress shall have Power To lay and collect Taxes, Duties, Imposts and Excises, to pay the Debts and provide for the common Defence and general Welfare of the United States; but all Duties, Imposts and Excises shall be uniform throughout the United States;

To borrow Money on the credit of the United States;

To regulate Commerce with foreign Nations, and among the several States, and with the Indian Tribes;

To establish an uniform Rule of Naturalization, and uniform Laws on the subject of Bankruptcies throughout the United States;

To coin Money, regulate the Value thereof, and of foreign Coin, and fix the Standard of Weights and Measures;

To provide for the Punishment of counterfeiting the Securities and current Coin of the United States;

To establish Post Offices and post Roads;

To promote the Progress of Science and useful Arts, by securing for limited Times to Authors and Inventors the exclusive Right to their respective Writings and Discoveries;

To constitute Tribunals inferior to the supreme Court;

To define and punish Piracies and Felonies committed on the high Seas, and Offences against the Law of Nations;

To declare War, grant Letters of Marque and Reprisal, and make Rules concerning Captures on Land and Water;

To raise and support Armies, but no Appropriation of Money to that Use shall be for a longer Term than two Years;

To provide and maintain a Navy;

To make Rules for the Government and Regulation of the land and naval Forces;

To provide for calling forth the Militia to execute the Laws of the Union, suppress Insurrections and repel Invasions;

To provide for organizing, arming, and disciplining, the Militia, and for governing such Part of them as may be employed in the Service of the United States, reserving to the States respectively, the Appointment of the Officers, and the Authority of training the Militia according to the discipline prescribed by Congress;

To exercise exclusive Legislation in all Cases whatsoever, over such District (not exceeding ten Miles square) as may, by Cession of particular States, and the Acceptance of Congress, become the Seat of the Government of the United States, and to exercise like Authority over all Places purchased by the Consent of the Legislature of the State in which the Same shall be, for the Erection of Forts, Magazines, Arsenals, dock-Yards, and other needful Buildings;--And

To make all Laws which shall be necessary and proper for carrying into Execution the foregoing Powers, and all other Powers vested by this

Constitution in the Government of the United States, or in any Department or Officer thereof.

Section. 9.

The Migration or Importation of such Persons as any of the States now existing shall think proper to admit, shall not be prohibited by the Congress prior to the Year one thousand eight hundred and eight, but a Tax or duty may be imposed on such Importation, not exceeding ten dollars for each Person.

The Privilege of the Writ of Habeas Corpus shall not be suspended, unless when in Cases of Rebellion or Invasion the public Safety may require it.

No Bill of Attainder or ex post facto Law shall be passed.

No Capitation, or other direct, Tax shall be laid, unless in Proportion to the Census or enumeration herein before directed to be taken.

No Tax or Duty shall be laid on Articles exported from any State.

No Preference shall be given by any Regulation of Commerce or Revenue to the Ports of one State over those of another; nor shall Vessels bound to, or from, one State, be obliged to enter, clear, or pay Duties in another.

No Money shall be drawn from the Treasury, but in Consequence of Appropriations made by Law; and a regular Statement and Account of the Receipts and Expenditures of all public Money shall be published from time to time.

No Title of Nobility shall be granted by the United States: And no Person holding any Office of Profit or Trust under them, shall, without the Consent of the Congress, accept of any present, Emolument, Office, or Title, of any kind whatever, from any King, Prince, or foreign State.

Section. 10.

No State shall enter into any Treaty, Alliance, or Confederation; grant Letters of Marque and Reprisal; coin Money; emit Bills of Credit; make any Thing but gold and silver Coin a Tender in Payment of Debts; pass any Bill of Attainder, ex post facto Law, or Law impairing the Obligation of Contracts, or grant any Title of Nobility.

No State shall, without the Consent of the Congress, lay any Imposts or Duties on Imports or Exports, except what may be absolutely necessary for executing it's inspection Laws: and the net Produce of all Duties and Imposts, laid by any State on Imports or Exports, shall be for the Use of the Treasury of the United States; and all such Laws shall be subject to the Revision and Controul of the Congress.

No State shall, without the Consent of Congress, lay any Duty of Tonnage, keep Troops, or Ships of War in time of Peace, enter into any Agreement or Compact with another State, or with a foreign Power, or engage in War, unless actually invaded, or in such imminent Danger as will not admit of delay.

Article. II.

Section. 1.

The executive Power shall be vested in a President of the United States of America. He shall hold his Office during the Term of four Years, and, together with the Vice President, chosen for the same Term, be elected, as follows:

Each State shall appoint, in such Manner as the Legislature thereof may direct, a Number of Electors, equal to the whole Number of Senators and Representatives to which the State may be entitled in the Congress: but no Senator or Representative, or Person holding an Office of Trust or Profit under the United States, shall be appointed an Elector.

The Electors shall meet in their respective States, and vote by Ballot for two Persons, of whom one at least shall not be an Inhabitant of the same State with them. And they shall make a List of all the Persons voted for, and of the Number of Votes for each; which List they shall sign and certify, and transmit sealed to the Seat of the Government of the United States, directed to the President of the Senate. The President of the Senate shall, in the Presence of the Senate and House of Representatives, open all the Certificates, and the Votes shall then be counted. The Person having the greatest Number of Votes shall be the President, if such Number be a Majority of the whole Number of Electors appointed; and if there be more than one who have such Majority, and have an equal Number of Votes, then the House of Representatives shall immediately chuse by Ballot one of them for President; and if no Person have a

Majority, then from the five highest on the List the said House shall in like Manner chuse the President. But in chusing the President, the Votes shall be taken by States, the Representation from each State having one Vote; A quorum for this purpose shall consist of a Member or Members from two thirds of the States, and a Majority of all the States shall be necessary to a Choice. In every Case, after the Choice of the President, the Person having the greatest Number of Votes of the Electors shall be the Vice President. But if there should remain two or more who have equal Votes, the Senate shall chuse from them by Ballot the Vice President.

The Congress may determine the Time of chusing the Electors, and the Day on which they shall give their Votes; which Day shall be the same throughout the United States.

No Person except a natural born Citizen, or a Citizen of the United States, at the time of the Adoption of this Constitution, shall be eligible to the Office of President; neither shall any Person be eligible to that Office who shall not have attained to the Age of thirty five Years, and been fourteen Years a Resident within the United States.

In Case of the Removal of the President from Office, or of his Death, Resignation, or Inability to discharge the Powers and Duties of the said Office, the Same shall devolve on the Vice President, and the Congress may by Law provide for the Case of Removal, Death, Resignation or Inability, both of the President and Vice President, declaring what Officer shall then act as President, and such Officer shall act accordingly, until the Disability be removed, or a President shall be elected.

The President shall, at stated Times, receive for his Services, a Compensation, which shall neither be increased nor diminished during the Period for which he shall have been elected, and he shall not receive within that Period any other Emolument from the United States, or any of them.

Before he enter on the Execution of his Office, he shall take the following Oath or Affirmation:--"I do solemnly swear (or affirm) that I will faithfully execute the Office of President of the United States, and will to the best of my Ability, preserve, protect and defend the Constitution of the United States."

Section. 2.

The President shall be Commander in Chief of the Army and Navy of the United States, and of the Militia of the several States, when called into the actual Service of the United States; he may require the Opinion, in writing, of the principal Officer in each of the executive Departments, upon any Subject relating to the Duties of their respective Offices, and he shall have Power to grant Reprieves and Pardons for Offences against the United States, except in Cases of Impeachment.

He shall have Power, by and with the Advice and Consent of the Senate, to make Treaties, provided two thirds of the Senators present concur; and he shall nominate, and by and with the Advice and Consent of the Senate, shall appoint Ambassadors, other public Ministers and Consuls, Judges of the supreme Court, and all other Officers of the United States, whose Appointments are not herein otherwise provided for, and which shall be established by Law: but the Congress may by Law vest the

Appointment of such inferior Officers, as they think proper, in the President alone, in the Courts of Law, or in the Heads of Departments.

The President shall have Power to fill up all Vacancies that may happen during the Recess of the Senate, by granting Commissions which shall expire at the End of their next Session.

Section. 3.

He shall from time to time give to the Congress Information of the State of the Union, and recommend to their Consideration such Measures as he shall judge necessary and expedient; he may, on extraordinary Occasions, convene both Houses, or either of them, and in Case of Disagreement between them, with Respect to the Time of Adjournment, he may adjourn them to such Time as he shall think proper; he shall receive Ambassadors and other public Ministers; he shall take Care that the Laws be faithfully executed, and shall Commission all the Officers of the United States.

Section. 4.

The President, Vice President and all civil Officers of the United States, shall be removed from Office on Impeachment for, and Conviction of, Treason, Bribery, or other high Crimes and Misdemeanors.

Article III.

Section. 1.

The judicial Power of the United States shall be vested in one supreme Court and in such inferior Courts as the Congress may from time to time ordain and establish. The Judges, both of the supreme and inferior Courts, shall hold their Offices during good Behaviour, and shall, at stated Times, receive for their Services a Compensation, which shall not be diminished during their Continuance in Office.

Section. 2.

The judicial Power shall extend to all Cases, in Law and Equity, arising under this Constitution, the Laws of the United States, and Treaties made, or which shall be made, under their Authority;--to all Cases affecting Ambassadors, other public Ministers and Consuls;--to all Cases of admiralty and maritime Jurisdiction;--to Controversies to which the United States shall be a Party;--to Controversies between two or more States;--between a State and Citizens of another State,--between Citizens of different States,--between Citizens of the same State claiming Lands under Grants of different States, and between a State, or the Citizens thereof, and foreign States, Citizens or Subjects.

In all Cases affecting Ambassadors, other public Ministers and Consuls, and those in which a State shall be Party, the supreme Court shall have original Jurisdiction. In all the other Cases before mentioned, the supreme Court shall have appellate Jurisdiction, both as to Law and Fact, with such Exceptions, and under such Regulations as the Congress shall make.

The Trial of all Crimes, except in Cases of Impeachment, shall be by Jury; and such Trial shall be held in the State where the said Crimes shall have been committed; but when not committed within any State, the Trial shall be at such Place or Places as the Congress may by Law have directed.

Section. 3.

Treason against the United States shall consist only in levying War against them, or in adhering to their Enemies, giving them Aid and Comfort. No Person shall be convicted of Treason unless on the Testimony of two Witnesses to the same overt Act, or on Confession in open Court.

The Congress shall have Power to declare the Punishment of Treason, but no Attainder of Treason shall work Corruption of Blood, or Forfeiture except during the Life of the Person attainted.

Article. IV.

Section. 1.

Full Faith and Credit shall be given in each State to the public Acts, Records, and judicial Proceedings of every other State. And the Congress may by general Laws prescribe the Manner in which such Acts, Records and Proceedings shall be proved, and the Effect thereof.

Section. 2.

The Citizens of each State shall be entitled to all Privileges and Immunities of Citizens in the several States.

A Person charged in any State with Treason, Felony, or other Crime, who shall flee from Justice, and be found in another State, shall on

Demand of the executive Authority of the State from which he fled, be delivered up, to be removed to the State having Jurisdiction of the Crime.

No Person held to Service or Labour in one State, under the Laws thereof, escaping into another, shall, in Consequence of any Law or Regulation therein, be discharged from such Service or Labour, but shall be delivered up on Claim of the Party to whom such Service or Labour may be due.

Section. 3.

New States may be admitted by the Congress into this Union; but no new State shall be formed or erected within the Jurisdiction of any other State; nor any State be formed by the Junction of two or more States, or Parts of States, without the Consent of the Legislatures of the States concerned as well as of the Congress.

The Congress shall have Power to dispose of and make all needful Rules and Regulations respecting the Territory or other Property belonging to the United States; and nothing in this Constitution shall be so construed as to Prejudice any Claims of the United States, or of any particular State.

Section. 4.

The United States shall guarantee to every State in this Union a Republican Form of Government, and shall protect each of them against Invasion; and on Application of the Legislature, or of the Executive (when the Legislature cannot be convened), against domestic Violence.

Article. V.

The Congress, whenever two thirds of both Houses shall deem it necessary, shall propose Amendments to this Constitution, or, on the Application of the Legislatures of two thirds of the several States, shall call a Convention for proposing Amendments, which, in either Case, shall be valid to all Intents and Purposes, as Part of this Constitution, when ratified by the Legislatures of three fourths of the several States, or by Conventions in three fourths thereof, as the one or the other Mode of Ratification may be proposed by the Congress; Provided that no Amendment which may be made prior to the Year One thousand eight hundred and eight shall in any Manner affect the first and fourth Clauses in the Ninth Section of the first Article; and that no State, without its Consent, shall be deprived of its equal Suffrage in the Senate.

Article. VI.

All Debts contracted and Engagements entered into, before the Adoption of this Constitution, shall be as valid against the United States under this Constitution, as under the Confederation.

This Constitution, and the Laws of the United States which shall be made in Pursuance thereof; and all Treaties made, or which shall be made, under the Authority of the United States, shall be the supreme Law of the Land; and the Judges in every State shall be bound thereby, any Thing in the Constitution or Laws of any State to the Contrary notwithstanding.

The Senators and Representatives before mentioned, and the Members of the several State Legislatures, and all executive and judicial Officers, both of the United States and of the several States, shall be bound by Oath or Affirmation, to support this Constitution; but no religious Test shall ever be required as a Qualification to any Office or public Trust under the United States.

Article. VII.

The Ratification of the Conventions of nine States shall be sufficient for the Establishment of this Constitution between the States so ratifying the Same.

The Word, "the," being interlined between the seventh and eighth Lines of the first Page, the Word "Thirty" being partly written on an Erazure in the fifteenth Line of the first Page, The Words "is tried" being interlined between the thirty second and thirty third Lines of the first Page and the Word "the" being interlined between the forty third and forty fourth Lines of the second Page.

Attest William Jackson Secretary

done in Convention by the Unanimous Consent of the States present the Seventeenth Day of September in the Year of our Lord one thousand seven hundred and Eighty seven and of the Independance of the United

States of America the Twelfth In witness whereof We have hereunto
subscribed our Names,

G°. Washington
Presidt and deputy from **Virginia** - **Delaware**, *Geo: Read, Gunning*
Bedford Jun, John Dickinson, Richard Bassett
Jaco: Broom, Maryland
James McHenry
Dan of St Thos. Jenifer
Danl. Carroll

Virginia
John Blair
James Madison Jr.

North Carolina
Wm. Blount
Richd. Dobbs Spaight
Hu Williamson

South Carolina
J. Rutledge
Charles Cotesworth Pinckney
Charles Pinckney
Pierce Butler

Georgia
William Few
Abr Baldwin

New Hampshire
John Langdon
Nicholas Gilman

Massachusetts
Nathaniel Gorham
Rufus King

Connecticut
Wm. Saml. Johnson
Roger Sherman

New York
Alexander Hamilton

New Jersey
Wil: Livingston
David Brearley
Wm. Paterson
Jona: Dayton

Pennsylvania
B Franklin
Thomas Mifflin
Robt. Morris
Geo. Clymer
Thos. FitzSimons
Jared Ingersoll
James Wilson
Gouv Morris

P. O. Box 2141
California City, CA 93504
760.373.8227 / 760.578.6258
Toll Free Fax: 877.842.3052
editor@ap4books.com

BIG THANKS!

Thank you to all who disagreed with me during exchange of ideas and countless conversations over the years. It was because of you that I wrote this book. You helped me to develop the possibilities that this book represents and suggests.

As always, appreciations go to my family for putting up with me during those countless dinners and social gatherings where I rant about this and that, I finally got it done gang.

Thank you also to my wonderful editor, Rosanne Mork, who never let me slide with anything that was half-hearted or written lightly. She always challenged me during the editing process and made me convince her that what I said and wrote about, I truly and honestly believed, even though at times she didn't agree with me or my approach.

Thank you also for my sounding board and great friend, Alan Bell. I have to convince him first, if an idea is going to fly.

Finally, thanks to my wife of fifty-one years, Lois, for listening when I woke her up in the middle of the night telling her of my ideas for this book; and for her patience during those many trips in the car when I reached for the radio to turn it down so that I could talk about my views on a number of subjects in this book. No one else could have put up with me. She always said, "Don't just tell me, put it in a book and hope people agree with you and don't think you're nuts." So I did.
I love you, Lois!

Elias Vidal

THE WAY IT ~~SHOULD~~ **MUST** BE

CONTACT THE AUTHOR DIRECTLY:

Lucho@ap4books.com

THE WAY IT ~~SHOULD~~ **MUST** BE